Fighting for your family has never
day and age! But what does fightin
you need to fight for them? And how do you fight for them? All these
questions and more are answered in this inspirational book. Filled with
endless truth from God's Word and heartwarming stories, I found "Fight
for your Family" to be both encouraging and motivating."

Shelley Switzer, Women's Ministry
Calvary Baptist Church, Taylorville Illinois

It's been said, "There is no greater ministry than your own personal
family." Jon Haley is a man that "Fights for His Family." In this book he
shows us a path that allows hustle and family health to co-exist. There is
no greater Fight than the Fight for your Family.

Brian Moore, Lead Pastor
Crosspointe Church, Anaheim, California

The family is the fundamental building block and basic unit of our society,
and its continued health is a prerequisite for a healthy and prosperous nation.
Is it still possible for a family to have a stable, nurturing environment?
Yes, but you have to fight for it. That's the focus of this book by Pastor Jon
Haley. It is filled with powerful and practical principles to help you win
this important battle. You will enjoy reading it.

Linzy Slayden, Lead Pastor
Friendship Baptist Church, Owasso, Oklahoma

I appreciated Jon Haley's challenge to fight for your family . . . not with
your family. He inspires parents to never give up. His section on love
languages was exceptionally helpful because he took the concepts and told
the stories of how they discovered and learned to speak their children's
love languages. I loved that they were so intentional in finding the keys to
their children's hearts. As parents, we all need to keep on learning and this
is a great resource!

Cindy Lyons, Women's Ministry
Highstreet Church, Springfield, Missouri

FIGHT FOR YOUR FAMILY: CAPTURING THE HEART OF YOUR CHILD

FIGHT

FOR YOUR

FAMILY

Capturing the ♥ of your child

JON HALEY

I want to dedicate this book on parenting to my parents. You both have been an encouragement and example of what it means to pursue Jesus. You have faithfully served your family and church well. Thank you for showing the four of us how to follow Jesus as you lead your family.

CONTENTS

FOREWORD

Choose your battles wisely!

Who isn't familiar with this truism? So, how is that accomplished? By choosing the prizefights that are important to you and your family's core values and by allowing the petty-minded skirmishes to pass through your "choosing" shredder. Small fights are for "small" fighters. Note them, but don't waste your time: because at times it is far better to achieve peace than to create carnage.

I have known the author longer than he has known me. His father and I attended the same college. I graduated a year earlier but Mike's reputation went before him, everywhere. He is the type of man whose word is his bond and his family is his life. The title of this book more likely is a heart's cry of this author's father. Look at his son and you will figure that out. He follows willingly and successfully in his father's footsteps. So it is almost like this book was a pre-determined project. Surely many of the words penned on its pages were learned in the laboratory of the Haley Family Compound. Pastors are familiar with a fight. They fight for the sheep God has chosen them to shepherd and they fight fiercely for the children God has chosen them to raise.

When the word fight is used in a sentence, generally a sobering thought will cross one's mind. If I enter into this fight, it is likely I will encounter some sort of pain in the process. The best of professional fighters know that though they may win the coveted belt, it will cost them pain. Maybe a black eye, a bloody nose, a swelled cheekbone or two, but the prize they will wear around their mid-section is worth the grueling pursuit. They understand there are two types of pain. One will hurt you. The other will change you. Pain will hurt you and make you more cautious. That same pain can make you a better fighter. You will step out of the ring a different warrior than when you entered.

And that is exactly what moms and dads are . . . warriors. Along with their common sense knowledge, they understand: children are our weapons. They are the arrows in our quivers. Arrows need honing. Your aim is critical. You have eighteen years to perfect it. The culture is the target. The battle is daily.

You may have to fight the fact that you find yourself illiterate when it comes to a biblical worldview. Fight to find role models for your children to watch and emulate. Fight your own urge to abdicate your responsibility to the church or local schoolteacher. Fight the deep feeling that you have a lifetime, so there is no urgency. Whatever the occasion, whatever the reason, get into this book and find out the why, where, when, and how of the fight.

Listen! Hear the cheers? Those are for you as you step into the ring to Fight for Your Family! Turn the page and face the challenge.

Dr. J. Otis Ledbetter

June 2020

ACKNOWLEDGEMENTS

My first acknowledgment is to my Lord and Savior, Jesus Christ. I have been blessed by God and am thankful for not only His saving grace but his sustaining grace in my life.

To my beautiful wife, Joy. You are my rock and the stability our kids needed. Our kids are blessed to have you as their Mother and I am thankful you joined me in the fight for our family. Thank you for your constant love, support, and encouragement.

To my kids, Blake and Blaire. Thank you for your motivation. You both have motivated me to always be the best man of God I can be. Thank you for accepting the many apologies for my failures as a Dad. I am blessed to have you two as my children.

To My Church, Hallmark has been a huge part of my family since 1997. I am who I am largely due to the men and women of Hallmark. I am grateful to serve here with an amazing body of believers. Thank you for the love and support you have given to me and my family.

To Amy Howard, the girl who I mercilessly picked on in youth group thirty years ago. God has miraculously brought our lives back together to bring this project to completion. Thank you for correcting my many mistakes.

INTRODUCTION

He felt the broken flesh around his eyes swelling but that was secondary to the gut-wrenching agony of realizing he had been defeated. He never got past that devastating night. Mike Tyson had lost to Buster Douglas! I have been in the ring with Mike Tyson. I grew up during the Atari 2400 era, which moved into the PlayStation and Nintendo systems. One of the most popular games on the Nintendo system, or at least, one of my favorite games came out in 1987. I was fourteen years old and loved to play *Mike Tyson's Punch Out*. It was an amazing game. Fighting Mike Tyson was the final challenge of the game. If you know anything about boxing, you have heard about Mike Tyson. He was a machine. He was knocking opponents out in the first round in what seemed like every fight. He was unstoppable. He was unstoppable in the game as well. He would knock you out with one punch. The game started as the player filling the role of Mac. Mac was a rookie fighter. The first fight was against Glass Joe. He did not have an impressive record. His record consisted of one win and ninety-nine losses. He heralded from Paris, France.

I wasted many hours in front of the television trying to beat that game. Eventually, I would win and then the game seemed pointless. In the real world, Mike Tyson would eventually lose to Buster Douglas and never really seemed to recover from the crushing defeat. Recently, ESPN aired a 30 for 30 entitled "Forty-two to One." The title is based on the odds Vegas placed on the fight. I don't have the space to explain the odds, but let's just say Vegas thought it would be a cold day in Hell before Buster Douglas would defeat Mike Tyson.

Let's move into a more modern fight story. Fast forward thirty years or so and you will hear about UFC. UFC stands for Ultimate Fighting Championship. The fight has now moved from the ring to the cage. The fights can be very brutal and gruesome. The champion this time is a woman. She, like Mike Tyson, seems unbeatable. Rhonda Rousey was a superstar. She had fame, power, money, and she could fight. She was undefeated and like Mike Tyson she was destroying her opponents. That was until November 14, 2015 in Melbourne, Australia. Holly Holm completely shocked the world when she completely destroyed Rhonda Rousey in very convincing fashion. Rhonda would never be the same again. She would soon retire from real fighting and move into the realm of staged wrestling.

Let me share with you a little of my fighting experience. I must confess I don't remember being in much of a real fight with anyone other than my brother. I have a twin brother and we got into a lot of fights over the years. Normally, we didn't hit each other in the face. We decided it wasn't worth getting into trouble and plus, it hurts. However, there were occasions when that treaty or pact was not honored. Typically, whoever was angrier at any given time was the one who would "win" the fight. The one with the most anger was the one who was more aggressive and thus the reason for the win. As I said, sometimes this pact to not hit in the face was broken. Let me share with you about one of those times. We were playing "dunk ball" in the church gym. The church my dad was a pastor of at that time. The gym had an eight-foot goal on the side. We would take turns trying to dunk on each other. One person would try to dunk while the other one tried to stand there and block the dunk. I don't exactly remember what happened, but a fight broke out. I got the best of him and even threw a nice karate kick to the side of his face. I knew I got him and I knew he was now very mad. However, he calmly stopped and said "let's just keep playing." He took his turn and I was a little passive on the block, still trying to make sure he wasn't angry. Everything went well. Now it was my turn to try and dunk it. Everything seemed good, but things were about to change. I took the two or three dribbles to get my momentum so that I could go up and dunk. I was about to get air born when he punched me square in the mouth. Blood went everywhere. He had completely split my bottom lip open. He immediately took off running. Strangely enough he didn't run out of the gym, but he ran into the kitchen. I chased him into the kitchen and found myself on top of the island, after ripping the fire extinguisher from the wall. Standing on the kitchen island in the middle of the church gym with a fire extinguisher in hand, the pastor's son was yelling wonderful four-letter words.

The goal of this book is not to inform you of great fights, fighters, or stories about me and my brother. I want to encourage you to fight for your family, not with your family. Satan has a goal to kill, steal, and destroy the family. He first started the fight in the Garden. God created the first family and placed them in the garden to have dominion over creation and to multiply. They were the first family and they were perfect. The earth was created in perfection and Adam and Eve only had one rule. They were not supposed to eat the fruit of one tree. Genesis 3 tells us about the first fight the family lost.

> Now the serpent was more cunning than any beast of the field which the Lord God had made. And he said to the woman, "Has God indeed said, 'You shall not eat of every tree of the garden'?"[1]

[1] Genesis 3:1 (NKJV)

Satan deceived her, and then convinced her, to take a bite of the forbidden fruit. So,

> when the woman saw that the tree was good for food, that it was pleasant to the eyes, and a tree desirable to make one wise, she took of its fruit and ate. She also gave to her husband with her, and he ate.[2]

This is the account of the first attack on the family and, unfortunately, Satan won the battle. Ten years ago, I completed the study, *The Quest for Authentic Manhood* by Robert Lewis.[3] He pointed out something in the verse that I had never seen before. Look back up and read it again. Do you see it? She also gave to her husband *with her*. What was Adam doing while Satan was deceiving her? God had told Adam not to eat and that if they did they would die. He passively sat there and let her be deceived. He chose not to fight for his family. He chose to be passive. I pray this book will encourage you to fight for your family. I don't have all the answers and I am not a licensed family planner. However, I am tired of watching families lose, and even more frustrated that families choose not to Fight.

---

[2] Genesis 3:6 (NKJV)
[3] Robert Lewis, *The Quest for Authentic Manhood* (Nashville, TN: LifeWay, 2003).

CHAPTER 1
A WORD OF WARNING

Before you start this fight, let me give you a warning. I believe, because you are reading this book, you have made a conscious decision to fight. I pray you have decided, like I have, that Satan is winning the battle in too many lives, homes, and families. I pray that God will place in you a desire to fight for your family. Fight for your wife, fight for your husband, fight for your kids, fight for your grandkids, fight for your finances, fight for your faith, fight for your purity; and the list could go on. One of my favorite stories in the Bible is the story of Nehemiah. Nehemiah was a Jewish man who was living in Persia. He was the cupbearer to King Artaxerxes. The main responsibility of the cupbearer was to make sure the food of the King was not poisoned. This was not a low position. This was not the case of having someone who was expendable taste the food before the King ate it. This was a position held by someone who was trusted by the King. The cupbearer was a trusted adviser to the King. He would have lived in the palace of the King. He lived as the King lived. I think I would enjoy this job. I would get to live like a King, in the palace of the King, without all the responsibilities of the King. Of course, it would only take one bad meal for the job to end.

Nehemiah, however, was not satisfied. He received news that the work of rebuilding the Temple, back home in Jerusalem had begun, but was not complete. He had also heard that the walls were destroyed. The walls laid in ruin. The walls were a testimony of the strength or the lack of strength of a city. The walls were a poor reflection of God as well. He loved Jerusalem and was anguished to see it in ruins, so he acted. He got permission to lead another wave of Israelites back to Jerusalem to rebuild the wall. Nehemiah did more than rebuild the wall, however; he also helped rebuild the spiritual life of the nation.

I am amazed that the men of the city and the other men in Persia would sit back and do nothing. They did not have a will to fight. They were okay with what had become normal. They were okay with the city not being protected. They were okay with simply being passive and choosing not to fight for their family or for their God. Unfortunately, I see this same apathy in our culture. I see many men and women unwilling to fight. I see many dads and moms satisfied with life as they know it. I see families who are struggling because they are not willing to fight for their family.

There are people who talk about doing something and then there are people who actually do something. Are you a person of action or words? Nehemiah chapter one reveals to us that Nehemiah had a passion to rebuild the wall. He was moved to action to rebuild the wall for the glory of God. He chose to fight for God's sake. Chapter two reveals barriers that will present themselves when you are moved to action. I pray, like Nehemiah, you will be moved to action. However, I also want you to be aware of a reality. When you decide to fight, Satan will fight back. When you decide to fight for the sake and glory of God, Satan will attack. The barriers found in chapter two are not limited to rebuilding a wall. I believe these barriers are present in almost every leadership decision. They are present in every decision that leads you to become a visible verbal follower of Jesus. Let me list them for you.

1. Comfort Zone

Jim Rohn puts it this way, "Your life does not get better by chance, it gets better by change." You can't stay where you are and go with God. You are going to have to make some changes and the first change is to get out of your comfort zone. Great things never come from your comfort zone. Nehemiah was comfortable. Nehemiah had everything. He had money, power, position and prestige.

He lived in the comforts of the palace. He chose to step out of his comfort zone and step into the fight.

2. Circumstances

Nehemiah 2:13-14, 17

[13] And I went out by night through the Valley Gate to the Serpent Well and the Refuse Gate, and viewed the walls of Jerusalem which were broken down and its gates which were burned with fire. [14] Then I went on to the Fountain Gate and to the King's Pool, but there was no room for the animal under me to pass. [17] Then I said to them, "You see the distress that we are in, how Jerusalem lies waste, and its gates are burned with fire. Come and let us build the wall of Jerusalem, that we may no longer be a reproach."[1]

The walls were way worse than he thought. The circumstances seemed insurmountable. How was he ever going to get the walls built? How would he get the funding? Would the King let him off? How would the King respond? There were so many barriers regarding his circumstances to list in this chapter. However, he chose to look past his circumstances and look towards God. I have heard it said, we tend to glance at God and glare at our circumstances;

[1] Nehemiah 2:13-14,17 (NKJV)

when we should glance at our circumstances and glare at God. God is bigger than your circumstances. Trust that God can work in you to win the fight.

3. Your Critics

We all have them. Nehemiah had received criticism from the enemy and from other Jews. They mocked him and told him it was an impossible task.

Nehemiah 4:1-3

[1] But it so happened, when Sanballat heard that we were rebuilding the wall, that he was furious and very indignant, and mocked the Jews. [2] And he spoke before his brethren and the army of Samaria, and said, "What are these feeble Jews doing? Will they fortify themselves? Will they offer sacrifices? Will they complete it in a day? Will they revive the stones from the heaps of rubbish-stones that are burned?" [3] Now Tobiah the Ammonite was beside him, and he said, "Whatever they build, if even a fox goes up on it, he will break down their stone wall."[2]

Nehemiah chose not to listen to his critics. He chose to follow the call of God on his life and disregard the noise. I

[2] Nehemiah 4:1-3 (NKJV)

love what he does. He goes to God and asks God to silence his critics.

Nehemiah 4:4-6

[4] Hear, O our God, for we are despised; turn their reproach on their own heads, and give them as plunder to a land of captivity! [5] Do not cover their iniquity, and do not let their sin be blotted out from before You; for they have provoked You to anger before the builders. [6] So we built the wall, and the entire wall was joined together up to half its height, for the people had a mind to work.[3]

You have been warned. The moment you make the decision to fight, Satan will fight back. As you decide to fight for your family I pray God will give you the strength to get out of your comfort zone, overcome your circumstances, and silence your critics.

---

[3] Nehemiah 4:4-6 (NKJV)

Chapter 2
For God's Sake Fight

Nehemiah chapter four gets to the good stuff. The picture of the movie Braveheart comes to mind. I am sure you know what I am talking about. Do you remember the famous battle scene? William Wallace, played by Mel Gibson, addressed the men who were terrified. They are looking across the battlefield at this formidable army and they say, "We are not going to fight. We are going to run, and live." Remember that scene? William Wallace, on that horse, was riding in front of them saying, "Men, they may take our life. But they will never take our freedom." His passion, his strength, his vision for what could be; empowered the men. Every time I watch that scene, I am ready to go to battle.

I loved that scene. When I saw it I could just picture our Lord, Jesus Christ, the captain of the armies of God riding that white horse, that white horse of Revelation 19, and saying to the men of God: "Will you fight? Men, will you fight for your wives? Wives, will you fight for your husbands. Will you fight for your sons? Will you fight for your daughters? Will you fight for your homes?" And I hope that you will stand up and say, "We will fight for our families."

I want to point out four things in chapter four that I pray will give you encouragement as you fight. I believe these four qualities allowed the men of Jerusalem to accomplish the goal of rebuilding the wall. These four qualities are transferable to us today as well. As you make the decision to fight for your family, I pray God will produce these qualities in your life.

1. A Mind to Work

Nehemiah 4:6

[6] So we built the wall, and the entire wall was joined together up to half its height, for the people had a *mind to work.*[1]

There were legitimate reasons to be afraid. There was a real enemy. The task of building the wall was huge. The circumstances were difficult and the critics were loud. These men of God didn't let that stop them. They had a calling on their life. They had made up their mind that God was in this and that God would fight with them. They made up their mind to do the work God called them to do.

---

[1] Nehemiah 4:6 (NKJV), italics mine.

I grew up in South Central Kansas. The winters seemed long and the summers were hot. I decided at the age of thirteen that I wanted to work. There were not a lot of options for a thirteen-year-old boy. My brother and I would collect aluminum cans and turn them in for a little money. We also mowed lawns in the neighborhood to earn a little cash. Along with my sister we threw the "Penny Power Paper" one day a week before school. This was no fun and now that I know the value of money it wasn't enough money either. My parents tried to teach us the value of working hard.

I decided the money from cans, lawns, and the paper route was not enough. I wanted to make some real money. The summer was upon us and I figured I could haul hay for one of the men at church. I am sure it wasn't that difficult. I was not very smart or very prepared. My dad helped me line it up. There was a man in the church who agreed to let me come work for him. It was a hot summer day. As I recall, it was the hottest day EVER recorded in the state of Kansas. That may not be accurate but that is what I remember. I knew from the first bail that I was in trouble. I was not as strong as I thought I was. Mowing lawns and throwing the paper early in the morning was a lot easier. I honestly can't remember how long we worked, but it seemed like it was all day. We went into the field and as the conveyer brought the bail to us we would use two hooks to grab the bail and then stack it on the truck. We would then enjoy the ride to the barn and unload every bail off the truck and restack it in the barn. This process would continue over and over for what seemed like eternity. I remember, like it was yesterday, one of the rides back to the field. I was tired. I was weak. I was hot. The man from church was driving the truck and he handed me a Tootsie Roll Pop. He said, "eat this you will get your energy back." He was wrong. However, to this day I rarely eat or see a Tootsie Roll Pop without thinking about that long hot summer Kansas day. I would like to be able to tell you that it got easier and I got stronger. The truth is, I never went back. I decided that I had enough money from the cans, the lawns, and the paper route. I guess I really didn't have a mind to work.

I don't share that story very often because I wish I would have stuck with it. I wish I would have kept trying. I wish I would have put in the time to get stronger and to make the money. If it was easy everyone would do it. I am sure you have heard that statement before. Fighting for your family is not easy.

After praying, Nehemiah and the Jews continued with the work. Some Christians pray and then wait for things to happen, but not Nehemiah! As in all his efforts, he blended the divine perspective with the human. He faced Sanballat's opposition with *both* prayer and hard work. Once he committed the problem to the Lord, he trusted God to help them achieve their goal. And while praying and trusting, they rebuilt the wall to half its height. At this juncture their task was half completed. Sanballat and Tobiah's efforts at demoralizing the Jews failed. The Jews rose above their enemies' attempts at discouragement. Because the people worked so diligently and enthusiastically (with all their heart), they were able to complete half the job in a surprisingly short period of time. Nehemiah wrote later (6:15) that the entire task was completed in 52 days (about eight weeks of 6 days each), so possibly this halfway point took about four weeks.[2]

The best thing to do is to pray and commit the whole thing to the Lord; and then *get back to your work!* Anything that keeps you from doing what God has called you to do will only help the enemy.[3]

---

[2] Gene A. Getz, "Nehemiah," in *The Bible Knowledge Commentary: An Exposition of the Scriptures*, ed. J. F. Walvoord and R. V. Zuck, vol. 1 (Wheaton, IL: Vicctor, 1985), 682.

[3] Warren W. Wiersbe, *Be Determined: Standing Firm in the Face of Opposition* (Colorado Springs, CO: David C. Cook, 1992), 53.

2. A Heart to Pray

Nehemiah 4:9

[9] Nevertheless we made our prayer to our God, and because of them we set a watch against them day and night.[4]

When we work, we work. When we pray, God works. I will be the first to admit that I do not feel my prayer life is where it should be. I need to pray more. I need to trust God more. I need to stop, be still, and know that He is God (Ps. 46:10). Prayer needs to be my first line of defense not my last resort. As Corrie Ten Boom famously asked, "Is prayer your steering wheel or your spare tire?" These men had a mind to work but also a heart to pray. They realized the task at hand was bigger than themselves. They realized that if this was going to be accomplished, it would be through the power of God.

Prayer brings the power of God in our lives. Bruce Ware said, "God has devised prayer as a means of enlisting us as participants in the work he has ordained, as part of the outworking of his sovereign rulership over all."[5] If we want to see mighty wonders of divine power and grace wrought in the place of weakness, failure and disappointment, let us answer God's standing challenge:

[4] Nehemiah 4:9 (NKJV)
[5] Bruce Ware, *God's Greater Glory: The Exalted God of Scripture and the Christian Faith* (Wheaton, IL: Crossway, 2004), XX.

Jeremiah 33:3

Call unto me, and I will answer thee, and show thee great and mighty things which thou knowest not![6]

The disciples asked Jesus to teach them to pray. This is powerful. As they experienced Jesus pray, they realized they needed to learn. As they hear him cry out and have a conversation with God the Father, it reveals their lack of prayer. It revealed their lack of ability to pray. They desired to pray like Jesus. Nehemiah prayed for God to give them the strength to accomplish what God had called him to do. Like Nehemiah we also need to pray. Dad, Mom, Husband, Wife; God has called you to fight for your family. God has called you to live a life of holiness and to be an example. You must have a mind to work and a heart to pray.

I have confessed already I am not great at praying and I am constantly trying to be better and work on my prayer life. Let me share with you a fairly common prayer tool that I use. I use the acronym A.C.T.S.

Adoration

Start your prayer by praising God. Praise God for who He is. He is your creator, your redeemer, your savior, your

[6] Jeremiah 33:3 (NKJV)

Lord. He has all power and wisdom. He is the King of Kings and the Lord of Lords. He is a God who knows, hears, sees, and cares.

Psalm 148:11-14

[11] Kings of the earth and all peoples; Princes and all judges of the earth; [12] Both young men and maidens; Old men and children. [13] Let them praise the name of the LORD, For His name alone is exalted; His glory is above the earth and heaven. [14] And He has exalted the horn of His people, The praise of all His saints—Of the children of Israel, A people near to Him. Praise the LORD![7]

Praise is simply complimenting God for who He is.

Confession

I think this one is easy to understand but hard to do. Confession is not saying, forgive all my sins I have committed, and will commit. It is not a generic blanket statement of asking God to forgive. Confession needs to be specific. God forgive me for having a bad attitude with my boss.

1 John 1:9

[9] If we confess our sins, He is faithful and just

---

[7] Psalm 148:11-14 (NKJV)

to forgive us our sins and to cleanse us from all unrighteousness.[8]

Take time each day to confess your sins and get back in alignment with God. As a believer, sin does not break our relationship with God, but it does break our fellowship with God. Confession leads us to unity and harmony with God.

Thanksgiving

You have plenty of reasons to be thankful. Thank God for His love, His faithfulness, His patience and a million other things. Express gratitude for what He's doing in your life. Thank Jesus for dying on the cross for you. Thank the Holy Spirit for indwelling you, and never leaving. Thank Him for being your conscience, your counselor, and that "still small voice."

Philippians 4:6-7

[6] Be anxious for nothing, but in everything by prayer and supplication, with thanksgiving, let your requests be made known to God; [7] and the peace of God, which surpasses all understanding, will guard your hearts and minds through Christ Jesus.[9]

[8] 1 John 1:9 (NKJV)
[9] Philippians 4:6-7 (NKJV)

1 Chronicles 16:34

[34] Oh, give thanks to the Lord, for He is good! For His mercy endures forever.[10]

Supplication

This was one that probably comes most naturally for us. We find it easy to tell God what we want. Do you really think any of your requests are big to God the Creator? Also, no request is too small for him.

Matthew 7:7-11

[7] "Ask, and it will be given to you; seek, and you will find; knock, and it will be opened to you. [8] For everyone who asks receives, and he who seeks finds, and to him who knocks it will be opened. [9] Or what man is there among you who, if his son asks for bread, will give him a stone? [10] Or if he asks for a fish, will he give him a serpent? [11] If you then, being evil, know how to give good gifts to your children, how much more will your Father who is in heaven give good things to those who ask Him!"[11]

I love this pattern of prayer. As I spend time praising God and acknowledge who He is and His holiness, I am

[10] 1 Chronicles 16:34 (NKJV)
[11] Matthew 7:7-11 (NKJV)

reminded of my wickedness. As I come into the presence of God, I have a deeper understanding of my sin. This was the response Isaiah had when he entered into the presence of God.

Isaiah 6:1-5

[1] In the year that King Uzziah died, I saw the Lord sitting on a throne, high and lifted up, and the train of His robe filled the temple. [2] Above it stood seraphim; each one had six wings: with two he covered his face, with two he covered his feet, and with two he flew. [3] And one cried to another and said: "Holy, holy, holy is the LORD of hosts; The whole earth is full of His glory!" [4] And the posts of the door were shaken by the voice of him who cried out, and the house was filled with smoke. [5] So I said: "Woe is me, for I am undone! Because I am a man of unclean lips, And I dwell in the midst of a people of unclean lips; For my eyes have seen the King, The LORD of hosts." [12]

Praise leads to confession. As I confess my sins and come into agreement with my sin and God's holiness I am reminded of how blessed I am. God, the creator of all things, hears my prayer. The God who spoke the world into existence by the power of his voice, listens to my

[12] Isaiah 6:1-5 (NKJV)

prayer. He forgives me for my sin. He is a God full of grace and mercy. I am humbled, thankful, and grateful that He chooses to forgive me. How blessed I am.

After I have praised the Lord, confessed my sins, and thanked Him for goodness I have a better perspective on what I should ask for. These steps help me align my will with His will. As I pray according to His will He will answer my prayers. A mind to work and a heart to pray are vital to having the will to fight.

3. An Eye to Watch

Nehemiah 4:9

[9] Nevertheless we made our prayer to our God, and because of them we set a watch against them day and night.[13]

They worked, prayed, and they watched. They watched with anticipation that the enemy could attack at any moment. This is great advice for you as you make the decision to fight for your family. When we move from talk to action, Satan also moves to action. Nehemiah was wise enough to expect the enemy to attack. The men prepared. They worked with one tool in their hand while holding a weapon in the other hand.

---

[13] Nehemiah 4:9 (NKJV)

Nehemiah 4:17-18

¹⁷ Those who built on the wall, and those who carried burdens, loaded themselves so that with one hand they worked at construction, and with the other held a weapon. ¹⁸ Every one of the builders had his sword girded at his side as he built. And the one who sounded the trumpet was beside me.[14]

As you fight, remember Satan will attack. Be on guard. Watch for him. Be ready. He will attack and He will be out to destroy you.

1 Peter 5:8

⁸ Be sober-minded; be watchful. Your adversary the devil prowls around like a roaring lion, seeking someone to devour.[15]

He is a roaring lion seeking whom he may devour. He is not trying to trip you up. He is not trying to get you a little confused. He is trying to destroy you and your family.

Ephesians 6:10-13

¹⁰ Finally, my brethren, be strong in the Lord and in the power of His might. ¹¹ Put on the whole armor of God, that you may be able to stand against

[14] Nehemiah 4:17-18 (NKJV)
[15] 1 Peter 5:8 (ESV)

the wiles of the devil. [12] For we do not wrestle against flesh and blood, but against principalities, against powers, against the rulers of the darkness of this age, against spiritual hosts of wickedness in the heavenly places. [13] Therefore take up the whole armor of God, that you may be able to withstand in the evil day, and having done all, to stand.[16]

Half the battle is knowing that you are in a battle. Work, pray, and watch because Satan will attack.

4. Faith to Fight

Nehemiah 4:20

[20] Wherever you hear the sound of the trumpet, rally to us there. Our God will fight for us.[17]

They knew if they had a mind to work, a heart to pray, and an eye to watch, God would fight for them. God is always at work for our good and for His glory. If God is for us then who can be against us? Greater is He who is in you than he that is in the world. God has called us to fight. God has called us to fight for our families. What He calls us to do He will empower us to accomplish. God will fight

---

[16] Ephesians 6:10-13 (NKJV)
[17] Nehemiah 4:20 (NKJV)

with you to accomplish His plan for you and His purposes in you.

Stop sitting in your comfort zone.
Stop listening to the critics.
Stop looking at your circumstances.
Start fighting for your family.

Here is the Braveheart Moment. Here is the Braveheart Verse.

Nehemiah 4:14

[14] And I looked, and arose and said to the nobles, to the leaders, and to the rest of the people, "Do not be afraid of them. Remember the Lord, great and awesome, and *fight for your brethren, your sons, your daughters, your wives, and your houses.*[18]

Nehemiah stood before the people and said, FIGHT FOR YOUR FAMILY! I pray, like the nation of Israel, you will FIGHT.

---

[18] Nehemiah 4:14 (NKJV) Italics mine.

CHAPTER 3
A MOTHER'S FAITH

My wife and I got married very young. I was nine days away from being twenty when we said "I do." Joy was three whole months into her second decade of life. We were in Bible college and we were in love. We didn't need money because we had love. The truth is we needed money, but all we had was love. God blessed us and we both graduated from college a few months before we celebrated our second wedding anniversary. We traveled for the summer representing our school, and in August of 1995 we started our first full-time vocational ministry position in Austin, TX. We enjoyed that first year of ministry and then decided we would begin trying to have a child. We found out in November of 1996 we were going to have a baby. I remember asking my young bride a really dumb question. Actually, I asked a lot of dumb questions. However, I asked her, will we know if our baby is ugly? I had watched Seinfeld and it seemed as if sometimes the parents were completely unaware that their child was not a pleasant site. There is an episode on Seinfeld in which everyone except the parents could see the baby was not, let's say attractive. Joy didn't like the question and I am pretty sure she never gave an answer. I told her I thought I would know. I thought I would be self-aware. Then it happened. July 14, 1997, I became a father. Blake Austin Haley was born. WOW! The moment we had been waiting for, the moment when I would know if he was cute or maybe not so cute, had arrived. I remember looking over him and thinking this poor boy has a face only his mother could love. He looked like an alien. He looked like he had lost his first fight. I think he had. He had this huge cone-shaped head and let's just say, my stupid question was answered, and I was very aware. Please don't stop reading. I feel you judging me right now. He got cleaned up and after a week or so, his head eventually took on a rounder shape. He was the most beautiful baby I had ever seen; until our daughter was born.

I will never forget my amazement at the birth of our two children. I was amazed at life and I was amazed at the strength of my wife. How blessed I was and still am to have an amazing woman in my life who has now given me a son and a daughter. My love for my kids was instant and my love for my wife grew even deeper at the birth of both of my children. There is no love like the love of a mother. There is no deeper connection than a mother and their child. I thank God for my mother, mother in-law and the great mother my kids have been blessed with.

Let's shift gears for a moment and take a look at one of the greatest mothers in history. This mom was a lady of great faith and great conviction. This mother was faithful to the Lord and trusted God with all she had. She had to make some tough decisions regarding her child, but ultimately, she knew God was the only one who could protect her son. God loves your child more than you do, and God has a greater ability to protect them and provide for them than you do. This mom had a child born under horrific circumstances. We find her story in Exodus.

Exodus 1:8-16

[8] Now there arose a new king over Egypt, who did not know Joseph. [9] And he said to his people, "Look, the people of the children of Israel are more and mightier than we; [10] come, let us deal shrewdly with them, lest they multiply, and it happen, in the event of war, that they also join our enemies and fight against us, and so go up out of the land." [11] Therefore they set taskmasters over them to afflict them with their burdens. And they built for Pharaoh supply cities, Pithom and Raamses.

[12] But the more they afflicted them, the more they multiplied and grew. And they were in dread of the children of Israel. [13] So the Egyptians made the children of Israel serve with rigor. [14] And they made their lives bitter with hard bondage—in mortar, in brick, and in all manner of service in the field. All their service in which they made them serve was with rigor. [15] Then the king of Egypt spoke to the Hebrew midwives, of whom the name of one was Shiphrah and the name of the other Puah; [16] and he said, "When you do the duties of a midwife for the Hebrew women, and see them on the birthstools, if it is a son, then you shall kill him; but if it is a daughter, then she shall live."[1]

The new King was afraid of the Israelites. They had become so many in number the King feared they would be overtaken. Therefore, the King decided he would have all the male boys killed. He ordered the Jewish midwives to kill all the boys during their birth. These Jewish midwives who did not have families of their own had a decision to make. They could value the life of these boys or value their own lives, but they could not do both. What choice

---

[1] Exodus 1:8-16 (NKJV)

would they make? They could choose to save the lives of the babies, but it would probably cost them their lives.

Exodus 1:17

[17] But the midwives feared God, and did not do as the king of Egypt commanded them, but saved the male children alive.[2]

They chose to defend the defenseless. America could learn a lot from these two ladies. These two Jewish women did not have families of their own but decided they would value the life of the babies even more than they would value their own lives. Their faith, their commitment, and their courage were unbelievable. They could be put to death for disobeying the order of the King.

Who we fear and respect the most, shapes the way we live our lives. Parenting is difficult, but in the process of parenting we must make a choice. We must decide who we are going to live for. Will we live in fear of what others think? Will we live in fear and cower to culture? Will we live in fear of God and raise our children to know and follow Him? These women chose to fear God more than the King. God would later bless these women with families of their own.

[2] Exodus 1:17 (NKJV)

The King decided to employ all of the Egyptians. He commanded them to throw all baby boys under the age of two into the river and let them die. At this point in the story, we read about the next hero. She is the mom of one of the most famous characters in all of the Bible. Her faith was amazing. We find her story in the second chapter of the book of Exodus, which her son wrote.

Exodus 2:1-2

[1] And a man of the house of Levi went and took as wife a daughter of Levi. [2] So the woman conceived and bore a son. And when she saw that he was a beautiful child, she hid him three months.[3]

Her name was Jochebed. Her name was not mentioned until later in the story. She was a lady of strong faith. We know she was a lady of faith because her story is listed in the chapter on the "Heroes of the Faith." Hebrews chapter eleven is known as the Hall of Faith.

Hebrews 11:23

[23] By faith Moses, when he was born, was hidden three months by his parents, because they saw he was a beautiful child; and they were not afraid of the king's command.[4]

[3] Exodus 2:1-2 (NKJV)
[4] Hebrews 11:23 (NKJV)

The faith of this mother led her to hide her son for three months. Her faith in God was greater than her fear of the King. That is a bold statement. Let me say that again. Her faith in God was greater than her fear of the King. Parenting is not easy. Parenting kids to know and follow God is not easy. Parenting requires faith. Parenting requires our faith in God to be larger than our fears. She hid him for three months, but as you know, babies are not quiet. The time came when she could no longer hide her little boy. She had a decision to make. She had to let her child go. She had come to the realization that God is the only one who could protect him. She could no longer protect her son and she must trust God to do what she could not do.

Exodus 2:3

[3] When she couldn't hide him any longer she got a little basket-boat made of papyrus, waterproofed it with tar and pitch, and placed the child in it. Then she set it afloat in the reeds at the edge of the Nile.[5]

WOW! Can you imagine what she was thinking? I cannot. I can't imagine laying my child in a handmade boat and laying him in the Nile River. I can't imagine what kind of faith that took. I can't imagine the emotions, fear,

[5] Exodus 3:2 (MSG)

and faith that led her to take this huge step of faith. She was helpless. She was desperate. She knew that unless God rescued him, he would die.

Have you ever heard someone say, the safest place for your child to be is in the center of God's will? Let me be transparent with you. I have said that. I said that to parents when they wouldn't let their student go on a mission trip with me because they were fearful. I had no business saying that. I was not in their situation and I was not even a parent. I would also contend that the statement is not accurate. Jesus was in the center of God's will and yet he was on the cross. I do believe if you change one word it would be a true statement. The *best* place for you to be is in the center of God's will. Jochebed believed the best place for her son to be was in the little boat on the Nile River.

The unknown scared the heart of this mom. She had Miriam, the older sister, hide and see what would happen. It seems as if Miriam was about six years of age at this time. She had two younger brothers. Aaron was three and Moses was three months old.

Exodus 2:5-8

[5] Then the daughter of Pharaoh came down to bathe at the river. And her maidens walked along the riverside; and when she saw the ark among the reeds, she sent her maid to get it. [6] And when

she opened it, she saw the child, and behold, the baby wept. So she had compassion on him, and said, "This is one of the Hebrews' children." [7] Then his sister said to Pharaoh's daughter, "Shall I go and call a nurse for you from the Hebrew women, that she may nurse the child for you?" [8] And Pharaoh's daughter said to her, "Go." So the maiden went and called the child's mother. [9] Then Pharaoh's daughter said to her, "Take this child away and nurse him for me, and I will give you your wages." So the woman took the child and nursed him.[6]

God didn't only save the boy. He allows Jochebed to nurse him. Not only does she get to nurse her own son, she gets paid to do it. The King's daughter is paying Moses' mom to take care of him. God blessed the faith of this mother and blessed her beyond what she could have ever imagined. God has a way of doing this. This mom had been riding a highly emotional rollercoaster. God's blessings are oftentimes on the other side of pain. God's biggest blessings often come after our biggest steps of faith. The faith of Jochebed does not end though. We will get back to this in a moment. For now, let's see if we can pull some

[6] Exodus 2:5-9 (NKJV)

application out from her amazing faith. In fact, let's look at three life lessons from the faith of Jochebed.

1. Believe God is Bigger than Your Problems.

Philippians 1:6

[6] being confident of this very thing, that He who has begun a good work in you will complete it until the day of Jesus Christ;[7]

Romans 8:28

[28] And we know that all things work together for good to those who love God, to those who are the called according to His purpose.[8]

Parenting is a constant test of our faith. We must constantly believe God is bigger than the problems we face. Jochebed seemed to face an insurmountable problem and yet she faced her fear with faith. She chose to believe that God was more powerful than the King. She chose to believe God could protect the son she could no longer protect. Remember, control is an illusion. You really are not in control and you must choose to believe God is and God can handle what you cannot.

[7] Philippians 1:6 (NKJV)
[8] Romans 8:28 (NKJV)

2. Choose to Follow God

Joshua 24:15

[15] And if it is evil in your eyes to serve the LORD, choose this day whom you will serve, whether the gods your fathers served in the region beyond the River, or the gods of the Amorites in whose land you dwell. But as for me and my house, we will serve the LORD."[9]

Matthew 6:33

[33] Seek the Kingdom of God above all else, and live righteously, and he will give you everything you need.[10]

Mom, Dad, who will you follow? Will God be the priority of your home? Will God be your first priority? Will God take the place over your career, family, and hobbies? Choose to follow God and lead your family to do the same. Jochebed chose faith over fear.

Following God will require two big steps. First, you must stop being selfish. We are by nature selfish people. We by nature take care of our needs before we take care of others. I am a poor father when I am selfish. I am a poor husband when I am selfish. I am a poor example of Jesus

[9] Joshua 24:15 (ESV)
[10] Matthew 6:33 (NLT)

when I am selfish. Secondly, you must daily take up your cross. This means you must daily deny yourself. You must daily make the choice to kill your selfish desires and follow God.

Matthew 16:24

²⁴ Then Jesus said to his disciples, "If any of you wants to be my follower, you must turn from your selfish ways, take up your cross, and follow me.¹¹

We must believe God is bigger than our problems and choose to follow him. The third lesson from Jochebed is not really another lesson. Well, maybe it is.

3. We Must be Prepared to Do it Again

Exodus 2:10

¹⁰ And the child grew, and she brought him to Pharaoh's daughter, and he became her son. So she called his name Moses, saying, "Because I drew him out of the water."

Jochebed placed Moses in the river and God protected him and gave him back to her. She was blessed to be paid to nurse her own son. However, she would have to give him back. She would have to choose faith over fear again. She

¹¹ Matthew 16:24 (NLT)

would have to surrender her boy once again to the control of God. She would once again come to the realization that God was the only one who could protect her son. She would hand her son back over to be raised by another lady. What a difficult decision. What remarkable faith this mom revealed.

Parenting parallels the realities of the Christian life. As a follower of Jesus, I must daily die to self and follow God. As a parent, I must daily surrender my kids to God and let Him have control. Tonight, I feel the pain of this decision. I feel the helplessness of not being in control. Currently, as I sit here in my home office and type this chapter, I realize how little control I have as a parent over the health and safety of my own kids. My daughter, Blaire, is nineteen years old and has just finished her first year of Bible college. Her major is Intercultural Studies. Joy, my wife, and I dropped her off at the airport today and she boarded a plane bound for Kenya, Africa. She will be serving an internship for a month in Kenya. God has blessed her and another college student from our church with this amazing opportunity. Today is a reminder that as a parent I must surrender my kids to God each and every day. I must, like Jochebed, have faith that is greater than my fears.

Jochebed had faith and released her son to the plans and purpose of God. Parent, let me encourage you to do the same. The *best* place for your child to be is in the center of God's will. Believe, trust, and do it again tomorrow. As Andy Stanley says, "Your greatest achievement to the Kingdom of God may not be something you do, but someone you raise." This mother of faith saved the baby that God would use to deliver the nation of Israel out of Egypt. Small steps of faith today may change the course of history tomorrow.

CHAPTER 4
LESSONS FROM DAD

I was blessed with a Dad and Mom who loved Jesus and, most of the time, they loved their kids. My dad, like many dads, loved fishing and hunting. My brother and I never really got into hunting, but we did take up fishing. I remember my dad taking my brother and I fishing one time and I learned some valuable lessons that day. Most of those lessons involved what not to do. My father decided to set trotlines on the local river. I wonder if you know what a trotline is. Let me briefly explain. A trotline is a line that you attach from one side of the river to the other. About every foot or so, you would have an additional line with a fishing hook attached to it. You tie one side of the line to a tree and it would drop into the water and then stretch it across the river and secure it to another tree. You then bait each hook and leave the line out all night. Sometimes we would stay up all night and go out and check the line every couple of hours to see if we had caught anything. Most of the time we went out with friends who owned a little row boat and we would get in the boat and check the lines by flashlight. However, if my dad is anything, he is cheap. Therefore, we did not own a boat. He had a brilliant idea one day to set the trotline by wading across the river. We set the line and baited the hooks and then went back to the cabin for the night with the plan of checking the line the next morning. My brother and I were about ten or eleven, if I remember correctly. I guess the river had risen over night and we didn't realize it. When I say we, I mean my dad. The river was flowing much faster and was much deeper than when we set out the line. My dad was checking the line and we were trying to help. However, the water was now over our chests and flowing very fast. We were no longer checking the line, but hanging on to the line while trying not to be swept away. I remember my brother crying, like a girl, in fear. I can't recall if I was or not. I wonder if my dad ever told my mom how serious it got on the water that day. Sorry Dad if you had not told Mom yet. The good news is we survived. Dad is about six foot and three inches tall. He had no problem standing in the "deep" water. He would reach out and grab our hand and pull us a little closer to the bank. I remember a real fear of dying that day. I also remember how the fear seemed to disappear when I was anchored to my dad. I knew that if I could hold on to his hand I would be okay. The security I felt in the strength of my dad's hand that day was palatable.

Dads, let me talk to you for a moment. The impact you have on your family is unbelievable. The responsibility you have to lead your family is undeniable. The opportunity you have to impact your kids is incomprehensible. Please, lead your family. We talked about Adam's failure to lead in the text earlier. Eve gave the fruit to him while he was with her. He passively stood by and watched Satan deceive his wife. He had been given the responsibility. He had been given the command not to eat of this tree. He was supposed to lead his wife.

Genesis 2:15-17

[15] Then the LORD God took the man and put him in the garden of Eden to tend and keep it. [16] And the LORD God commanded the man, saying, "Of every tree of the garden you may freely eat; [17] but of the tree of the knowledge of good and evil you shall not eat, for in the day that you eat of it you shall surely die." [18] And the LORD God said, "It is not good that man should be alone; I will make him a helper comparable to him."[1]

Do you see the timeline presented in these verses? God created man and then gave *him* the instruction. God told Adam he could eat of every tree except the Tree of

---

[1] Genesis 2:15-19 (NKJV)

the Knowledge of Good and Evil. He also warned if he ate the fruit of that tree he would surely die. Notice verse eighteen. After He gave the instructions, he made Eve. After the command was given to Adam, God created Eve. Adam was the one responsible to lead his wife to follow the Lord. Men, Dads, Husbands; it is your responsibility to lead your family. You need to be the security they can depend on when the water of life gets a little fast and a little high. There is a story in the New Testament of a dad who did exactly that. A dad who was willing to do whatever it took to lead his family well.

Luke 8:40-48

[40] So it was, when Jesus returned, that the multitude welcomed Him, for they were all waiting for Him. [41] And behold, there came a man named Jairus, and he was a ruler of the synagogue. And he fell down at Jesus' feet and begged Him to come to his house, [42] for he had an only daughter about twelve years of age, and she was dying. But as He went, the multitudes thronged Him. [43] Now a woman, having a flow of blood for twelve years, who had spent all her livelihood on physicians and could not be healed by any, [44] came from behind and touched the border of His garment. And immediately her flow of blood

stopped. [45] And Jesus said, "Who touched Me?" When all denied it, Peter and those with him said, "Master, the multitudes throng and press You, and You say, 'Who touched Me?' [46] "But Jesus said, "Somebody touched Me, for I perceived power going out from Me." [47] Now when the woman saw that she was not hidden, she came trembling; and falling down before Him, she declared to Him in the presence of all the people the reason she had touched Him and how she was healed immediately. [48] And He said to her, "Daughter, be of good cheer; your faith has made you well. Go in peace."[2]

Hit pause in the story for a moment. Don't pass over what has just taken place. Jairus's daughter was about to die. He was a leader who humbles himself to find Jesus and ask Jesus to heal his daughter. He was a ruler in the synagogue. You may not be aware of this, but the leaders in the synagogue were not big fans of Jesus. He didn't care at this moment. He knew his daughter was about to die and he was willing to do whatever it took to get his daughter healed. He fought his way through the crowd and got to Jesus. He fell on his face in humility before Jesus and begged Jesus to heal his twelve-year-old daughter.

[2] Luke 8:40-48 (NKJV)

He had eventually gotten to Jesus. He had finally asked Jesus to heal his daughter and then some lady interrupted him. Some lady touched the robe of Jesus and pulled his attention away from Jairus and his daughter. Put yourself in his shoes and feel his emotions. He was a desperate dad seeking Jesus to heal his daughter, knowing she is about to die. How would you feel? What would you do? How would you respond?

I believe every parent has had that moment when you would do just about anything to protect or provide for your child. I remember when my son was about two years old, he somehow reached up and grabbed the iron off of the ironing board and placed it on his hand. Joy called me in a panic and I immediately left work and sped home. They both jumped into the car and we quickly drove to the hospital. He was in severe pain and was so little. My heart hurts right now as I think about his pain. His entire palm was one huge blister. He did not know how to relieve or cope with his pain and so he kept biting it. I was hurting watching him hurting.

The three of us ran into the emergency room and he was screaming. I was in blackout mode. Joy patiently told the person at the desk we needed to see a doctor. The clerk handed her a clipboard and said, "Take a seat and fill this out." I said, very nicely I am sure, "Do you see his hand? We are not going to take a seat. We want to be in a room and see a doctor right now!" The clerk looked startled, but jumped up and walked us back to see a doctor. Every parent knows that feeling that wells up within you to protect and provide for your family. Jairus seemed to be much more patient and much more kind than I would have been. I would have made a scene I am sure. Let's look at the very next verse of the story.

Luke 8:49

49 While he was still speaking to her, a messenger arrived from the home of Jairus, the leader of the synagogue. He told him, "Your daughter is dead. There's no use troubling the Teacher now."[3]

How would you have responded at this point? I hate to admit it but I may have attacked that lady who had just been healed. Jesus may have healed her of one bleeding problem, but I would have given her another one. She cost Jairus his one chance to have his twelve-year-old daughter healed. She cost him the few minutes that could have changed his daughter's life forever. Before you get too angry or upset with the lady let's go back to the story.

[3] Luke 8:49 (NLT)

Luke 8:50-56

[50] But when Jesus heard it, He answered him, saying, "Do not be afraid; only believe, and she will be made well." [51] When He came into the house, He permitted no one to go in except Peter, James, and John, and the father and mother of the girl. [52] Now all wept and mourned for her; but He said, "Do not weep; she is not dead, but sleeping." [53] And they ridiculed Him, knowing that she was dead. [54] But He put them all outside, took her by the hand and called, saying, "Little girl, arise." [55] Then her spirit returned, and she arose immediately. And He commanded that she be given something to eat. [56] And her parents were astonished, but He charged them to tell no one what had happened.[4]

She was healed. She was brought back to life. The impact of the faith of this dad brought his daughter back to life. What kind of man was Jairus? We know he was a leader in the synagogue, but what does that mean?

Jairus was a leader of the local synagogue. The synagogue was the local center of worship, and Jairus was a lay person elected as one of

[4] Luke 8:50-45 (NKJV)

the leaders. The leaders were responsible for supervising worship services, caring for the scrolls, running the daily school, keeping the congregation faithful to the law, distributing alms, administering the care of the building, and finding rabbis to teach on the Sabbath.[5]

The ruler of a synagogue was the elder in charge of the public services and the care of the facilities. He saw to it that people were appointed to pray, read the Scriptures, and give the sermon. He presided over the elders of the synagogue and was usually a man of reputation and wealth. It took a great deal of humility and courage for Jairus to approach Jesus and ask His help, for by this time the Jewish religious leaders were plotting to kill Him.[6]

Jairus sounds like a man we should emulate. He sounds like a father a daughter could follow. I wonder what her name was. I wonder why we aren't given her name. Let's call her Julie, that daughter of Jairus. Julie grew up with a dad who loved the Lord. She grew up with

[5] Bruce B. Barton, Grant R. Osborne, Linda Chaffee Taylor, and David Veerman. *Luke*. Life Application Bible Commentary (Wheaton, IL: Tyndale House, 1997), 220.

[6] Warren W. Wiersbe, *Be Compassionate: An Expository Study of Luke 1-13* (Wheaton, IL: Victor, 1988), 112.

a sad person who fought for her family. She grew up with a dad who was willing to do whatever it took to protect her. Let's look at some qualities of Jairus we should also strive to acquire.

1. He Took the Initiative to Lead Physically

He could have sent someone after Jesus. He could have sent his wife. He could have been passive, but he was not. He chose to lead with actions. He engaged in the process of leading his family. Men, don't be passive. Be involved. Lead with action. Lead by being involved. Adam was passive and it cost him everything. Jairus led physically and had a huge impact on his family.

2. He Took the Initiative to Lead Spiritually

He went to Jesus. This is a great lesson for all of us. When we have a problem, take it to Jesus. Julie had a dad who was not afraid to lead spiritually. Families are desperate for men to spiritually lead their homes. Wives are desperate for men to spiritually lead their homes. Churches are desperate for men to lead their home. Learn from the example of Jairus and lead your home spiritually. Your kids need to see and hear you praying. Your kids need to see you read your Bible. Your kids need to see you actively engaged in your church services.

3. He Took the Initiative to Lead Emotionally

Jairus fell on his face and worshipped Jesus. He was passionate about his faith. He was passionate to introduce his family and his daughter to Jesus. Dad, please lead your home emotionally as well. Hang on, don't put the book down. I don't mean emotionally as in touchy, feely, and full of tears. I am talking about passion. Passion to love and follow Jesus. Your kids know what hobby you are passionate about. Do they know you have passion for Jesus?

Julie had a dad who pursued Jesus. Your family needs a dad who pursues Jesus. Dad, what do your children see in you? Do they see a dad who is not ashamed to seek the Lord? Do they see a dad who is not ashamed to bring Jesus into the house? Do they see a dad who prays for them and commits them into the hands of the Lord?

Michael Craven, in a post entitled, "Fathers: Key to Their Children's Faith," discusses a "study conducted by the Swiss government in 1994 and published in 2000 revealed some astonishing facts with regard to the generational transmission of faith and religious values." He explains:

The religious practice of the father of the family that, above all, determines the future attendance at or absence from church of the children.

The Study reports:

1. If both father and mother attend regularly, 33 percent of their children will end up as regular churchgoers, and 41 percent will end up attending irregularly. Only a quarter of their children will end up not practicing at all.

2. If the father is irregular and mother regular, only 3 percent of the children will subsequently become regulars themselves, while a further 59 percent will become irregular. Thirty-eight percent will be lost.

3. If the father is non-practicing and the mother regular, only 2 percent of children will become regular worshippers, and 37 percent will attend irregularly. Over 60 percent of their children will be lost completely to the church!

What happens if the father is regular but the mother irregular or non-practicing? Amazingly, the percentage of children becoming regular goes up from 33 percent to 38 percent with the irregular mother and up to 44 percent with the non-practicing. This suggests that loyalty to the father's commitment grows in response to the mother's laxity or indifference to religion.

In short, if a father does not go to church, no matter how faithful his wife's devotion, only one child in 50 will become a regular worshipper. If a father does go regularly, regardless of the practice of the mother, between two-thirds and three-quarters of their children will become churchgoers (regular and irregular). One of the reasons suggested for this distinction is that children tend to take their cues about domestic life from Mom while their conceptions of the world outside come from Dad. If Dad takes faith in God seriously then the message to their children is that God should be taken seriously.[7]

Dad, take your responsibility and Fight for your family

---

[7] S. Michael Craven, "Fathers: Key to Their Children's Faith," *Christian Post*, June 19, 2011, https://www.christianpost.com/news/fathers-key-to-their-childrens-faith.html.

CHAPTER 5
GIVING YOUR KIDS STRAIGHT A'S

Don't let the title fool you. I am not referring to grades in school. I will be completely honest with you; my family is not a straight A family. I did not get straight A's as a kid, my wife did not make straight A's, and neither one of our kids did. I believe there are four things we need to give our kids and if we do these four things we are being faithful to raise our kids as God would have us raise them.

I was fifteen when my family moved from Kansas to Texas. I was not happy. In fact, I was very angry. I resented them moving us across the country. I resented God for calling my dad away from our home to West Texas of all places. I mean who wants to move to Sweetwater, Texas? However, God knew this was the best thing for me and for my family. I remember one Sunday morning sitting in the youth group when a new kid walked in. My youth pastor told me to go introduce myself to the new kid. I reluctantly did. I sat down beside him and then invited him to join us for pizza that night. Little did I know we would become great friends.

Why do you need to know this story? Maybe a better question is, why did I choose to write this story? His parents did not make him go to church. His parents did not even come to church with him. We did not grow up in the same type of environments. His parents will not celebrate their fiftieth wedding anniversary this year, like my parents will. However, he is one of the godliest men I know. He has lived his life to train his family to love and follow Jesus. I am proud to call him friend and I am proud of the man he has become. He is an amazing husband, father, and leader in his church. He and his wife have several kids and have also adopted kids from the foster system. I respect him more than he knows. He grew up completely different than I did. I grew up in the home of a preacher. My family was not perfect, but we had a stable home and my parents did their best to point me to Jesus.

I want to be clear about what I am saying and what I am not saying. I don't believe there is a guarantee on our kids choosing to follow Jesus. I have been in full-time vocational ministry for nearly twenty-five years. I have grown up in church my entire life. I have observed a lot of family dynamics in those years. I have seen families who seemingly did everything they could to raise their kids to love Jesus, but their kids chose a different path. I have seen families who neglected their role to teach and train their children to follow Jesus who have kids who love Jesus.

Proverbs 22:6

[6] Train up a child in the way he should go, And when he is old he will not depart from it.[1]

Proverbs 22:6 is not a promise, but a principle. There is no promise that if you do these four things your kids will never mess up and they will become committed followers of Jesus. Parenting is stewardship. God has entrusted parents with kids and He has given us principles to follow. They are principles, not promises. We are to teach and to train, but ultimately every child has to make their own decision to follow Jesus or not to follow Jesus. The point is simple: there is no fail safe for raising kids. We are simply supposed to be wise stewards of what God has entrusted us. Wise stewardship is the goal as a parent. *Ultimately, we must answer to God on how we raised our kids, not on how they turned out.*

Single parent, let me be an encouragement to you. I realize the best case is for kids to have a dad and a mom and for both to be living out a godly example. However, just as there is no exact formula that works every time, there is not a formula that can't work either. Let me say on behalf of most churches and mine, I am sorry. I am sorry we have failed to engage you like we should. I am sorry we have not been a better support to you and your kids.

[1] Proverbs 22:6 (NKJV)

I am sorry churches are primarily designed for married couples. I don't have all the answers and my church still needs to improve and do a better job of understanding and supporting you, but please forgive us. Also, statistics are only statistics. The job you do to provide for your family is monumental. I am humbled by your dedication, faithfulness, and ability to fulfill both roles well. Remember what the Bible says about those who are without a parent.

Psalm 68:4-5

[4] Sing praises to God and to his name! Sing loud praises to him who rides the clouds. His name is the LORD—rejoice in his presence! [5] Father to the fatherless, defender of widows—this is God, whose dwelling is holy.[2]

Single parent, hang in there. God is on your side. God is fighting for you. God will honor your faithfulness and your commitment to train your kids to follow Jesus.

Let me share with you the four A's that you need to be sure and give to your children. Remember, there are no guarantees, but I believe some great principles. Here are the four things we need to strive to give our kids.

[2] Psalm 68:4-5 (NLT)

Matthew 17:1-6

[1] Now after six days Jesus took Peter, James, and John his brother, led them up on a high mountain by themselves; [2] and He was transfigured before them. His face shone like the sun, and His clothes became as white as the light. [3] And behold, Moses and Elijah appeared to them, talking with Him. [4] Then Peter answered and said to Jesus, "Lord, it is good for us to be here; if You wish, let us make here three tabernacles: one for You, one for Moses, and one for Elijah." [5] While he was still speaking, behold, a bright cloud overshadowed them; and suddenly a voice came out of the cloud, saying, "This is My beloved Son, in whom I am well pleased. Hear Him!" [6] And when the disciples heard it, they fell on their faces and were greatly afraid.

This was an amazing moment for Jesus. This is known as the transfiguration of Jesus.

There Jesus **was transfigured** (metemorphōthē "changed in form"; cf. Rom. 12:2; 2 Cor. 3:18) **before** this inner circle of disciples (Matt. 17:2). This was a revelation of Jesus' glory. The radiance of His glory was evidenced in **His face** and in His garments that **became as white as the**

light. Moses and Elijah appeared from heaven in some visible form and talked **with Jesus** (thus demonstrating that conscious existence follows death). Luke wrote that Moses and Elijah talked with Jesus about His coming death (Luke 9:31).[3]

Obviously, this was a huge monumental moment in the life of Jesus. I believe the four "A's" that we need to give our kids are found in one verse. They are exactly what God the Father did for God the son.

Matthew 17:5

[5] While he was still speaking, behold, a bright cloud overshadowed them; and suddenly a voice came out of the cloud, saying, "This is My beloved Son, in whom I am well pleased. Hear Him!"[4]

The four things we see God do are found in four words that start with the letter A. Therefore, the title straight A's. Here are the things we must give our children.

1. **Attention**
2. **Affection**
3. **Appreciation**
4. **Affirmation**

[3] Louis A. Barbieri, Jr., "Matthew," in *The Bible Knowledge Commentary: An Exposition of the Scriptures*, ed. J. F. Walvoord and R. B. Zuck, vol. 2 (Wheaton, IL, Victor, 1985), 59.
[4] Matthew 17:5 (NKJV)

I want to spend the next four chapters unpacking these four words. I believe if we can honestly and consistently give our kids these four things, we will be faithful to the responsibility of raising kids God has given to us. Remember the goal is to be wise stewards of what God has entrusted to us. Do not forget, we will answer to God on how we raised our kids, not on how they turned out.

Chapter 6
Attention

"Did you see me?" I am sure, if you are a parent, you have heard that phrase over and over. I am confident that if you have a young child, you hear that daily. When my two kids were younger, I heard that early and often. Another phrase I heard very frequently was, "Daddy, watch me." My kids wanted me to see every little thing they did. They might be jumping in the "deep end" and say before every jump, "Daddy, watch me." They would jump and then ask, "Did you see me?" There is something in every child who wants to be seen and heard. There is something in every kid that desires for people to be involved in what they are doing. Every kid desires to have attention on them.

Let's be honest, that desire doesn't seem to go away, it just manifests itself differently. Facebook, Instagram, and Twitter have brought this reality to life. There are numerous studies on the physiological effects that someone liking your post on Facebook has on you. We all like to be seen and heard. Our Facebook posts are as if we are saying

"Mom, Dad, watch me; did you see me?" We all crave attention. We all crave to be seen and heard.

20/20 recently aired an episode called *Screen Time,* revealing the amount of time we all spend looking at screens. Diane Sawyer reported American adults spend the equivalent of forty-nine days a year on their phone and tablets. She also reported that as games like *Fortnite* and *Overwatch* explode in popularity, the average teen gamer now spends almost twelve hours a week playing video games. The episode shows kids as young as two trying to get their parents attention as they mindlessly stare into their screens. One of the expert psychologists said, "the kids see our phones as an intruder and that they realize the phone is taking their parent away from them." The video shows babies who can barely walk inserting themselves in between their parent and the phone. One baby picked up a rattle and tried to divert her mom's attention from the phone. In the report, I heard one of the most powerful and impactful statements from one of the founders of an artificial intelligence company called Boundless Mind. Dalton Combs, a neurobiologist said, "There are only a few things that are finite. Attention is finite and it is basically the only finite thing that is left. The war over human attention is going to intensify."[1] Melinda Gates, the wife of Bill Gates, said "We have to be on top of it as parents

---

[1] abcnews.go.com/nightline/video/letting-phone-child-62797697

so they have real conversations with people and they can empathize with others not just be on their phones."[2]

I am forty-five years of age currently. I will soon be forty-six. My two kids are "grown." I have a son who is a month from being twenty-two and our daughter is nineteen. I can't fathom that my kids are "grown." I can't completely comprehend that they are officially raised. The time went so quickly. I have heard it said, the days seem long, but the years are short. Robert Lewis the author of *The Quest for Authentic Manhood* says there are three types of parenting.

1. Absent Parenting
2. Engaged Parenting
3. Strategic Parenting[3]

I hope this book helps you become a parent who is strategic in your parenting. Your kids crave and need your attention.

Matthew 17:5

[5] While he was still speaking, behold, a bright cloud overshadowed them; and suddenly a voice

---

[2] abcnews.go.com/nightline/video/letting-phone-child-62797697

[3] Robert Lewis, *The Quest for Authentic Manhood* (Nashville, TN: LifeWay, 2003).

came out of the cloud, saying, "This is My beloved Son, in whom I am well pleased. Hear Him![4]

God the Father gives us this amazing plan of practical parenting in one short verse. God the Father gives God the Son his attention. He shows us He is not absent. He is present. This moment, in the life of Jesus, was huge. God the Father showed up and gave God the Son attention. Parent, please show up. Parent, please be engaged with your child and what they are doing. Show interest in what they do. Make a sacrifice to be there and to be present and give them your attention when you are there.

Deuteronomy 6:3-9

[3] Listen obediently, Israel. Do what you're told so that you'll have a good life, a life of abundance and bounty, just as God promised, in a land abounding in milk and honey. [4] Attention, Israel!

GOD, our God! GOD the one and only!

[5] Love GOD, your God, with your whole heart: love him with all that's in you, love him with all you've got!

[6] Write these commandments that I've given you today on your hearts. Get them inside of you [7] and then get them inside your children. Talk

---

[4] Matthew 17:5 (NKJV)

about them wherever you are, sitting at home or walking in the street; talk about them from the time you get up in the morning to when you fall into bed at night. [8] Tie them on your hands and foreheads as a reminder; [9] inscribe them on the doorposts of your homes and on your city gates.[5]

The orthodox Jewish confession of faith is called "the Shema" after the Hebrew word which means "to hear." This confession is still recited each morning and evening by devout Jews all over the world, affirming "Jehovah, our Elohim, Jehovah is one." So important is this confession that Jewish boys in orthodox homes are required to memorize it as soon as they can speak. The nations around Israel worshiped many gods and goddesses, but Israel affirmed to all that there is but one true and living God, the God of Abraham, Isaac, and Jacob.[6]

This is the passage of scripture that Jesus quoted when the religious leaders asked him what is the greatest of the commandments. Jesus said the greatest commandment was to love God. He then added that we should love

---

[5] Deuteronomy 6:3-9 (MSG)

[6] Warren W. Wiersbe, *The Wiersbe Bible Commentary: The Complete Old Testament in One Volume* (Colorado Springs, CO: David C. Cook, 2007), 318.

our neighbor as ourselves. I want to take a minute to focus on the instructions given regarding the responsibility of parents in verse seven. There are assumptions made in this verse that I am not sure we can assume anymore.

Deuteronomy 6:7

> [7] and then get them inside your children. Talk about them wherever you are, sitting at home or walking in the street; talk about them from the time you get up in the morning to when you fall into bed at night.[7]

The assumption is that you will be spending time with your kids throughout the day. The verse was written to a culture that was completely different from the culture in which our kids are being raised. The culture was agricultural. The families did everything together. The kids learned by working alongside their mom or dad. They needed to work for their survival. I grew up in a family with three other siblings. My mom cooked a meal for the entire family each morning when I was younger. We might have poached eggs and toast. We may even have pancakes and bacon. To this day I can't eat pancakes without peanut butter. My mom would cook a full breakfast every morning and then a full dinner almost every night. She cooked real food too.

[7] Deuteronomy 6:7 (MSG)

We would have chicken fried steak with mashed potatoes and gravy or fried chicken with corn and green beans. Our family would sit around the table and talk every night. The dinner was also one of the greatest opportunities for us to learn conflict resolution because seemingly we always got into a fight at the dinner table. The point is, we sat together. We spent time together. Unfortunately, many families today don't do either of these. I am thankful for my wife who made a choice to not work full-time when our kids were at home. I was blessed to come home from work to a home cooked meal almost every night of the week. Sometimes this was a quick meal as we were usually headed out for either football, cheerleading, or basketball practice. However, Joy and I made a point to spend time with our kids at the dinner table.

I understand our culture is different and this is why it is so important that you become intentional. Your kids and your spouse need attention and if you don't give it to them, they will get it from someone or something else. The other day our kids were home from college and they both wanted homemade pizza. You know why they were craving homemade pizza? One of the reasons is obvious, it is good. However, the other, not so obvious reason, was because good memories are attached to homemade pizza. Friday night was movie and pizza night at our house. I would make the dough and spread it out on the pizza pans.

I am a little OCD and want it done a certain way. The kids would then come put the toppings on. They would sometimes make a face. The smile would be made out of pepperoni and the hair with sausage. They loved to put the toppings on and eat their homemade pizza. We would then sit down and watch a movie together. I suffered through a lot of bad movies on Friday night. I would not change a thing though.

I love golf and used to play all the time. However, when we had kids my weekly golf outing went from weekly to yearly. I used to take my day off and go golfing. I decided that my day off would be for family instead. The other day I was ordering a meal from McAlister's and the lady taking my order said, "Are you Blake's Dad?" I said, "Yes." She said, "You used to push me in the swings after lunch at recess." I kind of recognized her. She said, "I used to call you monkey ears." I definitely remembered her at this point. I do have big ears and kids are brutally honest. I used to go to the kids' elementary school every Friday and eat lunch with them. I would eat lunch and then go out to the playground after lunch and push all the kids in the swing. I would then go back into the lunchroom and eat with my other child and then make my way back out to the playground and push their class on the swings.

I want to share with you one last illustration before we close out this chapter. Jerry Seinfeld had a show on

Netflix entitled *Comedian in Cars Getting Coffee.* I have not watched a lot of the episodes but one of them caught my attention. The particular episode that was very intriguing was with comedian Howard Stern. I am not recommending you watch the show or even this particular episode, but Howard Stern revealed something about this childhood that was powerful. He was talking about trying to get the attention of his father and was not succeeding. His dad was preoccupied with listening to the radio in the car. I don't remember the entire story, but he revealed that the radio had his father's attention that he was craving to have. Here are the words of Howard Stern remembering back forty plus years to not getting attention from his dad.

> This is where it all started for me this radio was everything to my father. He would ignore me the entire time. I became enamored with the radio. I could get my father's attention if I could get in that box and get on the radio. The radio was the way of getting my Dad's attention.[8]

Howard Stern is one of the most famous radio personalities of all time. His net worth is reported by celebritynetworth.com as 650 million dollars. He built his career on the need to get his father's attention. His story is amazing.

[8] Comedians in Cars Getting Coffee, "The Last Days of Howard Stern," Netflix, Season 3, Episode 7, February 6, 2014.

He was so motivated to get his dad's attention that it set the trajectory of his life's work.

God the Father showed up for God the Son and you should do the same. Put the phone down and throw the ball with your kid. Put your iPad down and have a tea party. Put the work away and make a pizza. Put this book down and go pray with your kids before they go to bed. Remember, your kids crave attention, and someone will give it to them. I hope it's you.

CHAPTER 7
AFFECTION

Similarly to attention, we all crave and need affection. We need to be loved and we need to love. You see this from a nine-day-old baby who longs to be cuddled to the ninety-three-year-old lady at my church who needs a hug from her pastor every Sunday. A handshake is not enough. We were created in love by a God who is love. He desires to love us and for us to love Him back. The Lord publicly announced that He loved His son.

Matthew 17:5

[5] While he was still speaking, behold, a bright cloud overshadowed them; and suddenly a voice came out of the cloud, saying, "This is My beloved Son, in whom I am well pleased. Hear Him![1]

[1] Matthew 17:5 (NKJV)

1 John 4:7-11

[7] My beloved friends, let us continue to love each other since love comes from God. Everyone who loves is born of God and experiences a relationship with God. [8] The person who refuses to love doesn't know the first thing about God, because God is love—so you can't know him if you don't love. [9] This is how God showed his love for us: God sent his only Son into the world so we might live through him. [10] This is the kind of love we are talking about—not that we once upon a time loved God, but that he loved us and sent his Son as a sacrifice to clear away our sins and the damage they've done to our relationship with God. [11] My dear, dear friends, if God loved us like this, we certainly ought to love each other.[2]

I received a text message from my daughter today with a video attached. The video was of her driving in Kenya, Africa. I was shocked that she actually made the decision to drive. I have been to Kenya and the driving is a little scary. She told me before she left that her host had let her know that she might have a chance to drive if she wanted to. I told her that would be awesome, but don't tell your mom. I have had the opportunity to make five different

---

[2] 1 John 4:7-11 (MSG)

trips to Kenya. I first went in 2009 with my church. I was able to go back in 2010 and take my Father with me. I went for the third year in a row in 2011 and took my Father and my son. Several years past and I finally got to go back in 2016 and was able to take my daughter who was sixteen at the time. In January of 2019, I was able to go for my fifth trip and take both my son and my daughter. This was an unforgettable trip to experience with them. I love Kenya. I love the people of Kenya. They are generous and loving people. Their native language is Swahili, but most of them speak English as well. However, I love learning new words and trying to communicate in their native tongue. I have a shirt that I love to wear while in Kenya. The front of the shirt is designed in the shape of the continent of Africa. The inside of the continent is filled with English words and how they are spoken in Swahili. The great part about the shirt is the words are written upside down. The design is meant for the person wearing the shirt to be able to look down and read the words most often used. I use it as a cheat sheet to speak to the Kenyan people.

I was able to go to China a few years ago to spend some time with good friends who own a coffee shop. They took us out into the village to experience what it is like in the hills of southern China. We drove several hours up into the mountains and were expecting to have an awesome meal prepared for us. The meal was delicious and the cultural experience was one I will never forget. After the meal we sat around a small fire to share life stories. We were asked to share our favorite Bible verse. As we would quote our verse in English and then wait for it to be translated, I was amazed. I would speak in English. The next person would then speak in Mandarin. The next person would then translate from Mandarin to Axi. The next person then translated from Axi to the local tribal language. The local villager would respond and then the process would go in reverse order. The language you hear over an extended period of time will be the language you speak. I will explain why that is important in a moment.

This chapter is supposed to be about affection or love. Let me get back to the subject at hand. Gary Chapman in his book *The Five Love Languages* speaks about five different love languages.[3] If you have not read the book I recommend you read it. I would also recommend you take the Love Language test. You find the test online at www.5lovelanguages.com. He has several different books with the same premise. The book I have is entitled *The Five Love Languages of Teenagers*.[4]

The basic premise of his book is that we all have a love tank. In order for us to be happy and fulfilled in life

[3] Gary Chapman, *The Five Love Languages: How to Express Heartfelt Commitment to Your Mate* (Waterville, ME: Thorndike, 2005).

[4] Gary D. Chapman, *The 5 Love Languages of Teenagers: The Secret to Loving Teens Effectively* (Chicago: Northfield, 2016).

we must feel loved. "Sociologists, psychologists, and religious leaders all agree that the most fundamental need of the teenager is to feel emotional love from the significant adults in their life."[5] I think it is important to note there is a difference between being loved and feeling loved. You, no doubt, love your kids, but do they feel loved? David Popenoe, professor of sociology at Rutgers University and co-chair of the Council on Families in America, wrote, "Children develop best when they are provided the opportunity to have warm, intimate, and enduring relationships with both their fathers and their mothers."[6] Psychologists Henry Cloud and John Townsend add, "'There is no greater ingredient of growth for your youngster than love.'"[7] And in *Lost Boys*, James Garbarino asked; "What tools does a boy have to make sense of his life if he has no sense of being loved and appreciated?"[8]

Matthew 22:36-40

[36] "Teacher, which is the great commandment in the law?" [37] Jesus said to him, "'You shall love the LORD your God with all your heart, with all

[5] Chapman, *The Five Love Languages*, 40.

[6] David Popenoe, *Life Without Father: Compelling New Evidence That Fatherhood and Marriage Are Indispensable for the Good of Children and Society* (New York: Martin Kessler, 1996), 191.

[7] Henry Cloud and John Townsend, *Boundaries With Kids: How Healthy Choices Grow Healthy Kids* (Grand Rapids: Zondervan, 1998), 46.

[8] Cited in, Chapman, *The Five Love Languages*, 41.

your soul, and with all your mind.' [38] This is the first and great commandment. [39] And the second is like it: 'You shall love your neighbor as yourself.' [40] On these two commandments hang all the Law and the Prophets."[9]

Jesus spoke about loving God with all your heart. He was quoting from the Shema, as we talked about in the previous chapter. He added, 'You should love your neighbor as yourself.' I would contest that your closest neighbor is your family. We are to love God with all of our heart and to love our neighbors (family) as ourselves. "Nothing is more important in parenting teenagers than learning how to effectively meet the teen's need for emotional love."[10]

The book goes on to explain the five different love languages. I will give you a brief overview of each of the five love languages that is found on the Five Love Languages website.

1. Words of Affirmation

Actions don't always speak louder than words. If this is your love language, unsolicited compliments mean the world to you. Hearing the words, "I love you," are im-

---

[9] Matthew 22:36-40 (NKJV)
[10] Chapman, *The Five Love Languages*, 42.

portant—hearing the reasons behind that love sends your spirits skyward.

2. Quality Time

In the vernacular of Quality Time, nothing says, "I love you," like full, undivided attention. Being there for this type of person is critical, but really being there—with the TV off, fork and knife down, and all chores and tasks on standby—makes your significant other feel truly special and loved.

3. Receiving Gifts

Don't mistake this love language for materialism; the receiver of gifts thrives on the love, thoughtfulness, and effort behind the gift. If you speak this language, the perfect gift or gesture shows that you are known, you are cared for, and you are prized above whatever was sacrificed to bring the gift to you.

4. Acts of Service

Can vacuuming the floors really be an expression of love? Absolutely! Anything you do to ease the burden of responsibilities weighing on an "Acts of Service" person will speak volumes. The words he or she most want to hear: "Let me do that for you."

5 Physical Touch

A person whose primary language is Physical Touch is, not surprisingly, very touchy. Hugs, pats on the back, holding hands, and thoughtful touches on the arm, shoulder, or face—they can all be ways to show excitement, concern, care, and love. Physical presence and accessibility are crucial, while neglect or abuse can be unforgivable and destructive.

Interestingly enough Joy, myself, and our two kids all speak a different love language. The first time I read the book it was amazing to me. Joy and I first read the original book *The Five Love Languages* to help us in our marriage. We were amazed and astonished by the findings in the book. We had an interesting time trying to figure out which language the other one spoke. My love language is words of affirmation. I crave to have people to tell me how awesome I am. This is a tough language for a pastor. I hear about what I am doing wrong more than about what I am doing correctly. Joy's love language is acts of service. Remember the statement, *It is not about whether you love the other person, but whether they feel loved.*

Naturally you speak the language you hear. Does that sound familiar? I speak English because that is the language I hear most often. The same is true for your love language. Joy and I both love each other, but she naturally spoke her love language to me, and I naturally spoke my love language to her. I may have received her acts of service as a nice gesture, but it didn't make me feel loved because she is speaking the wrong language. I was quick to tell her how beautiful she was and how great the meal she prepared was, but I was not speaking her language of love. I was speaking mine. I was being nice, and she was grateful for my words of affirmation, but it didn't make her feel loved. I hope you understand then how important it is for you to know and to speak the love language of your spouse and your children.

I remember when our kids were little, Joy and I took the test to figure out what love language our kids spoke. We were both surprised to find out that neither of our kids spoke the language we did. Blake's love language was and still is Quality Time. Blaire's love language was and still is Receiving Gifts. As we answered the questions about them and began to process their love languages, it became very clear to us what language they spoke. Knowing the correct language is half the battle. As you learn what language they hear, you now have to adjust and speak their language.

Blake's love language was pretty obvious after we read the book. He has always been attached to me. He wanted to be where I was. If I was watching football, he wanted to be watching football. If I was playing softball, he wanted to play softball. I used this to my advantage and actually to his too. He was four when I convinced him to ask Santa Claus to give him a PlayStation 2 for Christmas. Santa Claus came through for me, I mean for him. Blake and I spent hours playing sports games on that PS2. It was a win for both of us. I got to play video games and he got to have quality time. He kills me in all of them now. High school was a little harder. He had friends who played the video games with him, and I wasn't good enough anymore. God blessed me with other avenues to spend time with him.

We moved to Kansas when he was in eighth grade. He did not like me very much for about a year or so. Quality time didn't happen a lot. I kept trying to figure out how to spend time with him. God provided a way. We moved into a new house and it had a hot tub on the back patio. I realized that he would actually talk to me out in the hot tub. I would go out there almost every night around ten or eleven. He would come out there often. He would talk sometimes and sometimes we would sit in silence for thirty minutes. We had a lot of meaningful conversations in that old hot tub. We also had a lot of stupid conversations in the hot tub. The point is we spent Quality Time soaking in the chlorinated waters on the back patio.

Blaire's love language is Receiving Gifts. You would think that would be easy, but it wasn't. We realized when she was very young that she loved getting gifts. We read the book and then realized when someone came into her room, she would explain what everything was and who gave it to her. Every little item on her cabinet had a story and a person attached to the story. She was in sixth grade and struggling. She was in a new school, new church, and in a new city. She was not happy with her dad and I couldn't really afford to get her a small gift every day to make her feel loved. What could I do every day to make her feel loved? What could I give her?

The school she attended blocked almost every app. I couldn't send her a note through Facebook or Twitter. Text messages didn't seem like much of a thought. I found out the school had not blocked Snapchat. Honestly, this was the one they should have been blocking, but they weren't. I set my alarm for 10:30 each morning. As I sat in my office, I would send her a Snapchat. Most of the time it was a funny statement with a funny face. I remember one that I sent her with a terrible face I was making. The caption said, "I am sorry, but genetics are strong." My phone would notify me when she opened it. Snapchat would also let me know when she would take a screenshot of the picture. I knew that when she took a screenshot the gift was received. Each time she opened the image, I was giving her a gift and she was feeling loved. Her emotional love tank didn't fill up overnight, but as I was making daily deposits, she slowly came back to us. I don't necessarily recommend Snapchat, but I will tell you it worked for me and my daughter.

Please make sure your kid feels loved. Josh McDowell says, "You can be the greatest explainer of the truth, but if the very heart of your son or daughter does not believe you love them, they will walk away from the truth." Remember the goal for them to feel loved. "People tend to embrace the teaching and beliefs of those who love them most. And your children are no different. They are much more likely to accept the truth you teach if you deliver it to them within a loving, heart-to-heart relationship."[11] I believe one of the keys to raising good children is to get their hearts early, keep their hearts, and be extremely vigilant not to lose their heart.

God blessed me in an unbelievable way with my son. I had the opportunity to coach him in all the sports he played when he was younger. He entered junior high and public schools and I assumed that I would no longer be able to coach him. However, God made a way. We moved to Kansas and during his last three years of high school I was blessed to be on the high school coaching staff. A memory I will cherish until I die is burned into my memory. I noticed that before each football or basketball game

[11] Stephen Kendrick, Lawrence Kimbrough, Randy C. Alcorn, and Alex Kendrick. *The Resolution: For Men* (Nashville, TN: B&H, 2011), 104.

he would go to the very back of the line as the team would line up for the national anthem. I took the opportunity to go stand behind him. Standing on the football field under the Friday night lights, he was watching the flag as I was watching him. As the crowd sang the national anthem, I would pray and thank the Lord for this special moment of quality time.

As Blaire got older, the Snapchat gift morphed into a mutual love for coffee. This would be the new gift I would give her. I will share a message from her Instagram which tells the story better than I can.

> Something that may come as a shock to you. I LOVE COFFEE. Wow you're shocked I know! Although I love the taste and smell of coffee there's a much more sentimental reason as to why I love coffee so much. Growing up there was one thing I remember so intensely; my dad would sit in his office, reading and obtaining as much knowledge as he possibly could from his Bible, while drinking a nice warm cup of coffee. Oftentimes, I would go into his office and make a cup of coffee, even though I could not stand the taste of it. Now why did I start drinking coffee if I didn't even like it? I made myself drink coffee because I wanted something that was special to

just my Dad and me. I wanted to be more like my Dad. My brother and my Dad both bonded over sports, but I was never into sports. So I began drinking more and more coffee just so I could go into my Dad's office and be with him. Although I would never admit this to him growing up, I loved to just watch my Dad in his office read his Bible and plan his sermons. I'm lucky and thankful to have the Dad that I was so graciously given; except when he wakes me up singing…but that's a whole different story. Eventually, I came to love coffee and now I can't go a day without it. Thanks Jon. My Dad and I started to bond over coffee more and more. It became our thing to surprise each other with Starbucks drinks. we would go to coffee shops together. We would try different coffees and try different ways to make it. When we would go on trips, we would buy each other coffee and coffee mugs. When I was sad, my dad would get me coffee. It was our special thing we shared. I know that this long childhood memory seems so pointless, but trust me I have a reason as to why I'm telling this. I made myself do something every single day in order to grow closer to my Dad to the point I now can't go a day without drinking coffee. I was striving to be more and more like my Dad. Something I realized is that I need to be doing this everyday with my Heavenly Father. God has so much for us and wants us to be in a relationship with him everyday. Not when we have a little free time. Not when we can squeeze Him in to our busy day for only a few minutes before bed. We should be spending everyday striving to be more and more like Him. We should be diving into His Word every single day doing our best to gain as much wisdom and knowledge as we can. Just as I can't go a day without coffee, we as Christians should come to the point where we can't go a day, an hour, or even a minute without reading God's Word, or simply talking and being in a relationship with Him. I know that coffee is so mundane to most, but to me it has become an important aspect of my life because it allowed me to grow closer to my dad. Gaining wisdom and knowledge of God's word and being in a relationship with my Heavenly Father should be even more crucial to my everyday life. I hope this encourages you to step back and evaluate how much you're striving to be more and more like the God who created you. The God who loves you enough to send His son to die in your place. Be in a relationship with Him everyday not just in your free time.

Kids are craving love and desperately in need of affection. Your kids will get it from someone or somewhere. I beg you to follow the example God gave us and give them affection privately and publicly. Do your homework and do everything you can to make them feel loved. They need to have your attention and they need your affection.

CHAPTER 8
APPRECIATION

Let's take a moment to review the verse that is driving our straight A conversation. Jesus is in the middle of a monumental moment in His life and God shows up. God the Father gives God the Son: Attention, Affection, Appreciation, and Affirmation.

Matthew 17:5

[5] While he was still speaking, behold, a bright cloud overshadowed them; and suddenly a voice came out of the cloud, saying, "This is My beloved Son, in whom I am well pleased. Hear Him!"[1]

God gives attention by being there. He then gives him affection by publicly stating His love for His Son. He reveals His appreciation for His Son by stating He is well pleased with him. The verse ends with a two-word sentence affirming Jesus.

[1] Matthew 17:5 (NKJV)

I believe every parent has asked the following question, "*What do you say?*" Let me ask you, "what do you say?" I am confident you answered with a short two-word answer. "Thank you!" I remember teaching this to our kids. I remember being taught these two words. I grew up being taught to answer everyone "Yes sir" and "Yes ma'am", and to say "Please" and "Thank You." I also tried to teach my two kids to respond to people in the same manner. I will tell you though, this didn't always work. I remember a parent fail at Christmas one year. Blake, our son, was about four and we had been trying to teach him to say thank you and to appreciate what he received. The real test would be how he would respond while opening up his Christmas presents. This may have been the same year I convinced him to ask Santa for a PlayStation 2. My sister, his Aunt Sissa, got him a gift. He had opened some other gifts already and of course we would echo, "What do you say?" He would respond with a polite "Thank You." However, what was about to come out of his mouth was not what we were hoping for. Let me preface this by saying Blake has always been into sports and pretty much only sports. He never really played with toy guns, blocks, cars, Legos; or any other child appropriate toy you could imagine. He simply played with sports equipment or any type of ball. He has never and really still is not into clothes. Ok, I feel like I am making excuses for him and maybe I am. He opens the gift from his Aunt and it is a shirt. I can still remember the look on his face, my wife's face and my sister's face after he responded. He picks up the shirt from the box and immediately throws the shirt to the floor and yells out, "BOOO PRESENT!" We had failed as parents. He did not show the proper appreciation for the gift he was given.

I wonder why it is so hard to get our kids to appreciate what they have been given. Is this because we all tend to not be content with what we have? I believe it is difficult to teach appreciation because it is not natural. Paul wrote he had learned to be content.

Philippians 4:10-13

[10] But I rejoiced in the Lord greatly that now at last your care for me has flourished again; though you surely did care, but you lacked opportunity. [11] Not that I speak in regard to need, for I have learned in whatever state I am, to be content: [12] I know how to be abased, and I know how to abound. Everywhere and in all things I have learned both to be full and to be hungry, both to abound and to suffer need. [13] I can do all things through Christ who strengthens me.[2]

[2] Philippians 4:10-13 (NKJV)

The action of learning leads me to think that contentment and gratitude are not instinctive. In fact, there is a story in the Bible that brings this point home really well.

Luke 17:11-19

[11] It happened that as he made his way toward Jerusalem, he crossed over the border between Samaria and Galilee. [12] As he entered a village, ten men, all lepers, met him. They kept their distance [13] but raised their voices, calling out, "Jesus, Master, have mercy on us!"

[14] Taking a good look at them, he said, "Go, show yourselves to the priests."

They went, and while still on their way, became clean. [15] One of them, when he realized that he was healed, turned around and came back, shouting his gratitude, glorifying God. [16] He kneeled at Jesus' feet, so grateful. He couldn't thank him enough—and he was a Samaritan.

[17] Jesus said, "Were not ten healed? Where are the nine? [18] Can none be found to come back and give glory to God except this outsider?" [19] Then he said to him, "Get up. On your way. Your faith has healed and saved you."[3]

[3] Luke 17:11-19 (MSG)

You would have expected all ten men to run to Jesus and thank Him for a new start in life, but only one did so—and he was not even a Jew. How grateful the men should have been for the providence of God that brought Jesus into their area, for the love that caused Him to pay attention to them and their need, and for the grace and power of God that brought about their healing. These men needed their mom to ask them, "What do you say?" I can't imagine the lack of gratitude. They had been given their lives back. They could now go see their families. They could go back to their jobs. They could hug their kids once again. They had everything to be grateful for and yet they chose not to appreciate the gift they had been given.

> But before we judge them too harshly, what is our own "GQ"—"Gratitude Quotient"? How often do we take our blessings for granted and fail to thank the Lord? Too often we are content to enjoy the gift but we forget the Giver. We are quick to pray but slow to praise.[4]

One out of ten came back and said thank you. I wonder if that percentage is an accurate representation of how many of us are grateful for the gifts God has given us. Do you have an attitude of gratitude?

[4] Warren W. Wiersbe and Ken Baugh. *Be Courageous: Take Heart from Christ's Example : NT Commentary Luke 14-24* (Colorado Springs, CO: David C. Cook, 2010), 64.

I believe we all struggle to be content and to have a spirit of appreciation. I believe this third A, which represents Appreciation, has a few more layers than the first two A's. I want to approach this from a slightly different perspective and angle than the first two. Let's look at three different ways in which we can give Appreciation to our kids.

Here are the three ways in which we can give Appreciation. First, we should be appreciative of the gift of our kids. Secondly, we need to appreciate the gift in our kids. The third aspect is to appreciate the season.

1. Appreciate the Gift of Your Kids

Psalm 127:3

[3] Behold, children are a heritage from the LORD,
The fruit of the womb is a reward.[5]

Children are a gift from the Lord. During those late nights and early mornings, we sometimes forget how blessed we are. The teen years can also be a time when we wonder if they really are a gift. I love the story of Hannah found in 1 Samuel. Hannah was desperate to have a child. She had prayed and prayed and God had not blessed her with a child. She went to the Temple of the Lord and prayed for God to give her a child.

[5] Psalm 127:3 (NKJV)

1 Samuel 1:8-11

[8] Then Elkanah her husband said to her, "Hannah, why do you weep? Why do you not eat? And why is your heart grieved? Am I not better to you than ten sons?"

[9] So Hannah arose after they had finished eating and drinking in Shiloh. Now Eli the priest was sitting on the seat by the doorpost of the tabernacle of the LORD. [10] And she was in bitterness of soul, and prayed to the LORD and wept in anguish. [11] Then she made a vow and said, "O LORD of hosts, if You will indeed look on the affliction of Your maidservant and remember me, and not forget Your maidservant, but will give Your maidservant a male child, then I will give him to the LORD all the days of his life, and no razor shall come upon his head."[6]

God answers her prayer and gives her a son. She acknowledges that her son is a gift of God. She had prayed for him and God blessed her with a son.

1 Samuel 1:20

[20] So it came to pass in the process of time that Hannah conceived and bore a son, and called his

[6] 1 Samuel 1:8-11 (NKJV)

name Samuel, saying, "Because I have asked for him from the LORD."[7]

As you raise your kids, you must continually remind yourself God has blessed you with a gift. God has entrusted you with a precious life and you must treasure the gift of your child. I feel as if this could come across as being very simple, but I do believe it will have a profound impact on your life and the life of your child. Parenting is complicated and very frustrating. If we are not conscious of the reality they are gifts of God, we oftentimes view them as burdens instead of blessings. The result of this attitude will be evident for your child. When we lose the sense of appreciation for the gift God has given us, it will be evident in our attitude, actions, and words.

Have you ever said, "I feel like a taxi driver?" Have you ever made a comment that you *have* to go to work in order to pay for their food, activities, etc.? Do you gripe as you drive them to school and home after school? Let's not even begin to talk about the pick-up line at school. Do your kids sense they are burdens or do they feel like blessings? Yesterday I saw a mother with a shirt that said, *"I can't, my kid has practice."* What message does that send to her child? What message are you sending to your child?

[7] 1 Samuel 1:20 (NKJV)

God has given you the gift of your children and let's be careful to appreciate the gift we have been given.

> Thank God for your children because they are the ones who grow you up into spiritual maturity. To the degree that your heart is overwhelmed with gratitude for your children, they will gain the core education they most need—the knowledge that they are truly loved, treasured, and delighted in. Only a genuinely thankful parent can invest in his or her children with the conviction that they are focused on unconditional love.[8]

Does your child know that you appreciate them? Do they feel appreciated, loved, and affirmed? God gifted you with your child, make sure they feel as if they are a blessing not a burden.

2. Appreciate the Gift in Your Kids

No two kids are exactly alike. I have an identical twin brother and we are not exactly alike. We are very similar, but we are different. We have different personalities and different gifts. My brother had a date in college with a girl and we got the brilliant idea to try and switch during the middle of the date. He took her bowling and halfway

---

[8] Dan B. Allender, *How Children Raise Parents: The Art of Listening to Your Family* (Colorado Springs, CO: Waterbrook, 2005), 4.

through the evening he excused himself to the bathroom. I was in the bathroom waiting for him to come in. He took his shirt off and I put it on. I walked out and the date resumed. She did not notice at first. However, about fifteen minutes into the switch she finally got the nerve to question me. She said, "Wait, are you Jon? I acted offended. I let her know I was upset that I had taken her out to eat and now paid for bowling and she didn't even know if I was Michael or Jon. She apologized and felt sincerely bad for hurting my feelings. I then confessed, and she kind of laughed. Neither one of us ever went on another date with her though. I wonder why? I finally asked her, "What made you realize I was Jon and not Michael?" She was reluctant to tell me. She finally said, "Your butt is bigger." Ha-ha, she was not wrong.

While in high school, we almost used our appearance to our advantage. I was much better in history class and he was much better in geometry. We had the same teacher, but at different times. The plan was for me to take his test and for him to take my test. We were both completely confident that the teacher would not know the difference. We were not as confident that a friend in class may notice and inadvertently say something that would get us caught. However, the biggest deterrent was that we did not trust each other. He was afraid that I would fail the test on purpose. We look a lot alike and even used to sound alike, but we are different. The point is, we are all uniquely created by God and we all have different gifts and abilities.

Psalm 139:13-14

[13] For You formed my inward parts; You covered me in my mother's womb. [14] I will praise You, for I am fearfully and wonderfully made; Marvelous are Your works, and that my soul knows very well.[9]

God created your kids with different personalities, different interests, and different gifts. You need to celebrate the differences, not compare them. We tend to prefer some gifts over other gifts. We tend to enjoy one child's abilities over another. This is natural in some cases. I love sports and my son loves sports and is very good at them. It was more natural for me to appreciate his gifting in athletics. I remember coaching Blake in soccer when he was three years old. He was motivated when I was tough on him. I could get on him pretty hard and it would inspire him to play even harder. I learned very early, while coaching Blaire, that she was different. I was coaching her in basketball for the first time when she was in kindergarten. She continually would catch the ball and then immediately pass it. She wouldn't dribble it or shoot it. I yelled to her across the court, "Blaire, you dribble the ball well, so dribble to the goal." She began crying on the court. I was shocked. I was stunned. I was at a loss for words. I called her over to the bench and apologized. We later had a conversation about what my role as her coach would look like moving forward.

Paul was a mentor to Timothy. We don't really hear much about Timothy's dad. Paul was definitely Timothy's spiritual father. He would address Timothy as his son in the two letters he wrote him. He would encourage, challenge, and inspire Timothy to be the young man that God had gifted him to be. The first few verses of the second letter Paul wrote to Timothy are powerful.

2 Timothy 1:1-7

[1] Paul, an apostle of Jesus Christ by the will of God, according to the promise of life which is in Christ Jesus, [2] To Timothy, a beloved son: Grace, mercy, and peace from God the Father and Christ Jesus our Lord. I thank God, whom I serve with a pure conscience, as my forefathers did, as without ceasing I remember you in my prayers night and day, [4] greatly desiring to see you, being mindful of your tears, that I may be filled with joy, [5] when I call to remembrance the genuine faith that is in you, which dwelt first in your grandmother Lois

and your mother Eunice, and I am persuaded is in you also. ⁶ Therefore I remind you to stir up the gift of God which is in you through the laying on of my hands. ⁷ For God has not given us a spirit of fear, but of power and of love and of a sound mind.¹⁰

Paul calls him a beloved son in verse two. Paul tells Timothy, in verse six, to stir up the gift God has given him. Paul acknowledged that God had gifted Timothy and he was encouraging him to continually perfect the gift God had blessed him with. Let me share verse six with you from another English translation.

2 Timothy 1:6

⁶ For this reason I remind you to fan into flame the gift of God, which is in you through the laying on of my hands.¹¹

Paul is trying to inspire Timothy to use the gift God has blessed him with. As a parent, you need to do the same. You need to see the gift God has blessed your child with and encourage them to use that gift. Several years ago, my brother and I were able to take both of our boys to the Philippines. They both love basketball and so do

¹⁰ 2 Timothy 1:1-7 (NKJV)
¹¹ 2 Timothy 1:6 (ESV)

my brother and I. We have a shared passion for sports. We had uniforms made and a missionary friend of ours set up basketball games all over the area in which we were visiting. We played a community all-star team. We played at a local university who had a lot of international students. We played a team made up of pastors. We played another team that was police officers and city councilmen. We had a blast. At each of the games, we would have a chance to talk about Jesus at half-time. I was blessed to share the love of sports with my son and watch my son use his gifts for Kingdom purposes. Oh and by the way, we only lost one game and that was to the university team.

Blaire was good at sports, but she didn't find as much enjoyment in them as Blake and myself. She is very gifted in art. She has an amazing ability in the art of graphite. In fact, she has partially funded two of her own mission trips through being commissioned to draw for individuals. Today as I type this, she is in Kenya teaching art to students. Yesterday she posted a picture of herself teaching a young boy how to do a self-portrait. As a parent, it is our job to help them find their gifts and help them use their gifts for building the Kingdom of Jesus. Celebrate the gifts of your children and don't compare them.

3. Appreciate Your Current Season

Paul said he had learned to be content. This means it is not natural. We must learn to be content. We must learn to have an attitude of gratitude. Although it is not natural, it is possible. Two verses after he wrote he had learned to be content, he wrote the words, "I can do all things through Christ who gives me strength" (Phil. 4:13, NKJV). This means contentment can be achieved. We can learn to be content in whatever situation in which we find ourselves.

Every parent has played the *I can't wait until* game. You have said it I am sure. This game begins very early. I can't wait until they are born. I can't wait until this baby learns to sleep. I can't wait until they walk. I can't wait until they talk. I can't wait until they go to Kindergarten. I can't wait until they can do their own homework. I can't wait until they drive. I think you get the point. We hurry the process and we are always looking and anticipating the next season will be better than the current season. This is beginning to sound like what it is like to be a Dallas Cowboys fan. We often fail to enjoy the present, looking toward the future.

I am sure you have heard or read the following quote. "The clock is running. Make the most of today. Time waits for no man. Yesterday is history. Tomorrow is a mystery. Today is a gift. That's why it is called the present." Enjoy the season you are in. My wife is an amazing person. She keeps our house clean, picked up, and looking great. When our kids were younger she would be frustrated that the sink was full of dishes, or the entry-way was full of dirty shoes. I would often say to her, one day you will miss the cluttered sink and messy house. Honestly, it wasn't that I had so much more wisdom or perspective than her, I didn't want to have to clean. The point is still relevant. Each season of parenting seems difficult. Each season of parenting is easy to wish away. We must learn to appreciate our current season.

I pray as we have unpacked the third A, which stands for Appreciation, you will work on having an attitude of gratitude.

Psalm 100:1-5

[1] Make a joyful shout to the LORD, all you lands! [2] Serve the LORD with gladness; Come before His presence with singing. [3] Know that the LORD, He is God; It is He who has made us, and not we ourselves; We are His people and the sheep of His pasture. [4] Enter into His gates with thanksgiving, And into His courts with praise. Be thankful to Him, and bless His name. [5] For the LORD is good;

His mercy is everlasting, And His truth endures
to all generations.[12]

Pause and thank God for the gift of your child, the gift in
your child, and your current season.

---

[12] Psalm 100:1-5 (NKJV)

CHAPTER 9
AFFIRMATION

I mentioned earlier I was a little OCD on some things. I believe everyone is OCD about something. I am OCD when it comes to my lawn and when it comes to carpet. The lawn must look good and it must be cut and trimmed perfectly. I have owned four houses and I have worked very hard on all of them to have a nice lawn. The most difficult yard I had was the backyard in Kansas. We had huge trees I had to keep trimmed in order for the grass to grow. I had to water, fertilize, and overseed. The lawn took several years to get it looking like I wanted it and when I did, I was proud of it. A friend of mine bought my house after we moved back to Texas. The backyard neighbor (we didn't have a fence) told him after a year of living there that he was glad he had a new neighbor. He said, "Jon used to make his backyard look so good and I felt bad that mine looked so bad." Apparently, the new owner is not OCD about the grass. Carpet is another area in which I am OCD. Thankfully for me the carpet in our house doesn't count. Let me explain. If you can see the lines in the carpet when you vacuum it then it has to be done a certain way. The carpet we have at home is so old that the lines can no longer be seen. The last church I pastored had a small sanctuary, but I would vacuum it every week so that the lines all went the right way. I would be upset if I showed up to church on Sunday morning and the lines were no longer visible. I usually vacuumed it again. Thankfully out of the 80,000 square feet in the church I serve now. There is only one little section in the sanctuary that lines are created when you vacuum. Yes, I know right where it is and I notice the lines every Sunday morning. Usually I walk around them so the lines will stay looking good. What does my obsession have to do with making our kids feel affirmed? Great question. I believe the reason that I am OCD in these two areas is a result of my parents words of affirmation. My OCD in this area speaks to the power our words have.

The words we speak to our kids have the power to direct, destroy, or delight. God the Father shows up when God the Son is getting baptized. This baptism will begin his earthly ministry and thrust Jesus into the purpose in which he came to fulfill God the Father speaks words of affection, appreciation, and affirmation. The last two words God the Father speaks affirms Jesus and His ministry.

Matthew 17:5

[5] While he was still speaking, behold, a bright cloud overshadowed them; and suddenly a voice came out of the cloud, saying, "This is My beloved Son, in whom I am well pleased. *Hear Him!*[1]

God the Father affirms his ministry by telling the crowd to listen to him. God the Father speaks to the validity of God the Son's ministry with two simple words, *Hear Him*! Do you see it? Do you get it? God is saying, this is my Son whom I love, appreciate and acknowledge that He is good and should be listened to.

> Both children and adults want the approval of and praise from their dads. They want their father's "blessing" in their lives. To bless means "to speak well of." When you bless your children, you are lovingly using your God-given authority to verbally affirm them toward future success.[2]

We often underestimate the power of our words. The words you speak to your children have the power of life and death. Please, Mom and Dad choose your words wisely.

[1] Matthew 17:5 (NKJV). Italics mine.
[2] Stephen Kendrick, Lawrence Kimbrough, Randy C. Alcorn, and Alex Kendrick. *The Resolution: For Men* (Nashville, TN: B&H, 2011), 111.

Let me share with you a few quotes and verses of scripture that speak to the power of your words. "Be mindful when it comes to your words. A string of some that don't mean much to you, may stick with someone else for a lifetime."[3]

Proverbs 15:1

[1] A gentle response defuses anger, but a sharp tongue kindles a temper-fire.[4]

Proverbs 15:4

[4] Kind words heal and help; cutting words wound and maim.[5]

Raise your words, not your voice. It is rain that grows flowers, not thunder.[6]

Proverbs 16:24

[24] Kind words are like honey—sweet to the soul and healthy for the body.[7]

Kind words can be short and easy to speak, but their echoes are truly endless.[8]

[3] Rachel Wolchin, https://www.inc.com/peter-economy/26-brilliant-quotes-on-the-super-power-of-words.html

[4] Proverbs 15:1 (MSG)

[5] Proverbs 15:3 (MSG)

[6] Rumi, https://www.inc.com/peter-economy/26-brilliant-quotes-on-the-super-power-of-words.html

[7] Proverbs 16:24 (NLT)

[8] Mother Teresa, https://www.inc.com/peter-economy/26-brilliant-quotes-on-the-super-power-of-words.html

Proverbs 18:20-21

[20]Wise words satisfy like a good meal; the right words bring satisfaction. [21]The tongue can bring death or life; those who love to talk will reap the consequences.[9]

Words are singularly the most powerful force available to humanity. We can choose to use this force constructively with words of encouragement, or destructively using words of despair. Words have energy and power with the ability to help, to heal, to hinder, to hurt, to harm, to humiliate and to humble.[10]

Do you remember the old saying from the playground, "Sticks and stones may break my bones, but words will never hurt me?" That is such a lie. This statement could not be farther from the truth. The power of words is mind-blowing. My parents knew that, I know it, and you know it. The power of the untamed tongue to damage those who we speak to is unimaginable.

Have you noticed the descriptions used for soap, shampoo, and body wash now? If you were to just read the descriptive words used to describe it would seem

[9] Proverbs 18:20-21 (NLT)

[10] Yehuda Berg, "The Power of Words," Huffington Post, September 14, 2010, https://www.huffpost.com/entry/the-power-of-words_1_b_716183.

that it should be something you eat or drink. Let me give you a few. "Pomegranate Lemon Verbena." What is that? Here is another, "Passion Struck Fuji Apple and Vanilla Orchid." I saw one that said, "Milk Shake with Organic Muru Muru." Again, is this body wash or something to drink? I can tell you from experience that soap is not to be consumed. Have you ever heard your parents or grandparents say, "You want me to wash your mouth out with soap?" I think that may be a thing of the past. I hope so. I do not recommend this as a parenting tool or as a diet plan. I remember sitting in the car as a young boy and calling my sister a name. The next thing I remember was being dragged to the bathroom and a bar of soap being shoved into my mouth. I gritted my teeth and quickly my teeth began to do the work of a cheese grater. The soap went pretty violently across my teeth as I was being told never to say that again. I tasted soap for the next few hours and sat in the back of the car calling my sister that name over and over in my head. The point is, my parents knew the power of my negative words. Not sure they understood the power of soap in my mouth. Maybe that is why I am tempted to try the new "scented" soaps. I mean they sound a lot better than a bar of Ivory soap.

When God spoke those words to Jesus, He spoke them publicly. He publicly praised His Son. He publicly affirmed the gifting of His Son. He publicly acknowledged that His Son was a great leader and should be listened to. Parents, your words are more powerful than you will ever know. The words you speak or don't speak have the power to direct, destroy and delight.

> The power of speech is one of the greatest powers God has given us. With the tongue, man can praise God, pray, preach the Word, and lead the lost to Christ. What a privilege! But with that same tongue he can tell lies that could ruin a man's reputation or break a person's heart. The ability to speak words is the ability to influence others and accomplish tremendous tasks; and yet we take this ability for granted.[11]

Warren Wiersbe says the tongue has the power to direct, destroy, and delight. I want my words to direct and delight not destroy.

1. Direct

James 3:1-4

[1] My brethren, let not many of you become teachers, knowing that we shall receive a stricter judgment. [2] For we all stumble in many things. If

[11] Warren W. Wiersbe, *The Wiersbe Bible Commentary: The Complete New Testament in One Volume* (Colorado Springs, CO: David C. Cook, 2007), 867.

anyone does not stumble in word, he is a perfect man, able also to bridle the whole body. ³ Indeed, we put bits in horses' mouths so that they may obey us, and we turn their whole body. ⁴ Look also at ships: although they are so large and are driven by fierce winds, they are turned by a very small rudder wherever the pilot desires.[12]

Both the bit and the rudder must overcome contrary forces. The bit must overcome the wild nature of the horse, and the rudder must fight the winds and currents that would drive the ship off its course. The human tongue also must overcome contrary forces. We have an old nature that wants to control us and make us sin. There are circumstances around us that would make us say things we ought not to say. Sin on the inside and pressures on the outside are seeking to get control of the tongue.[13]

Your words have the power to direct your children.

Studies conducted by Dr. John Cacioppo of the University of Chicago have shown what he calls "the negative bias" of the brain. Negatives have a much greater impact on our brain. Our brains

[12] James 3:1-4 (NKJV)

[13] Wiersbe, *The Wiersbe Bible Commentary*, 867.

are actually more sensitive and responsive to unpleasant news and remarks. That's why personal insults or criticism hit us harder and stay with us longer. Our brain contains a built-in partiality toward negative information.[14]

2. Destroy

James 3:5-8

[5] Even so the tongue is a little member and boasts great things. See how great a forest a little fire kindles! [6]And the tongue is a fire, a world of iniquity. The tongue is so set among our members that it defiles the whole body, and sets on fire the course of nature; and it is set on fire by hell. [7] For every kind of beast and bird, of reptile and creature of the sea, is tamed and has been tamed by mankind. [8] But no man can tame the tongue. It is an unruly evil, full of deadly poison.[15]

Your words have enormous power to destroy people. They have even greater power to destroy your children. The problem is that we can't tame our tongue without changing our heart. The Bible says out of the abundance of a man's heart he speaks. In other words, our words are

[14] Peggy Bert, http://www.peggybert.com/2010/09/30/positive-and-negative-words/

[15] James 3:5-8 (NKJV)

a sign of our heart. I can't just will myself to not say negative words. You can start with that, but you need to get the
root of the issue. You need to get to the heart of the matter.
"God understands that the conduct of a man will never
outperform the content of his character, because conduct
is an expression of character."[16]

Let me share with you three steps to overcome negative words.

• Renew Your Mind

Romans 12:1-2

[1] I beseech you therefore, brethren, by the mer-
cies of God, that you present your bodies a living
sacrifice, holy, acceptable to God, which is your
reasonable service. [2] And do not be conformed to
this world, but be transformed by the renewing of
your mind, that you may prove what is that good
and acceptable and perfect will of God. [17]

[16] Stephen Arterburn, Kenneth L. Luck, and Mike Yorkey, *Every
Man, God's Man: Every Man's Guide to Courageous Faith and Daily
Integrity* (Colorado Springs, CO: WaterBrook, 2003), 40.
    [17] Romans 12:1-2 (NKJV)

- **Guard Your Heart**

  Proverbs 4:23

  [23] Guard your heart above all else, for it determines the course of your life.[18]

- **Change Your Thinking**

  Philippians 4:8-9

  [8] Finally, brethren, whatever things are true, whatever things are noble, whatever things are just, whatever things are pure, whatever things are lovely, whatever things are of good report, if there is any virtue and if there is anything praiseworthy—meditate on these things. [9] The things which you learned and received and heard and saw in me, these do, and the God of peace will be with you. [19]

Your words can direct, destroy and thirdly they can delight.

3. Delight

  James 3:9-12

  [9] With it we bless our God and Father, and with it we curse men, who have been made in the

[18] Proverbs 4:23 (NLT)
[19] Philippians 4:8-9 (NKJV)

similitude of God. [10] Out of the same mouth proceed blessing and cursing. My brethren, these things ought not to be so. [11] Does a spring send forth fresh water and bitter from the same opening? [12] Can a fig tree, my brethren, bear olives, or a grapevine bear figs? Thus no spring yields both saltwater and fresh.[20]

Let's go back to the carpet and the grass. I remember like it was yesterday my mom telling me how good I vacuum. I remember as a young boy seeing the lines in the carpet and my mom pointing out how good I was at it. As you know, my love language is words of affirmation. As she was telling me how good I was doing, I was feeling affirmed. The power of those words of affirmation spoke to a young boy and now forty years later still have an impact. Yes, mom I now know you were bragging so that I would do it again. This does not negate the power of words. When I was in high school we lived in the church parking lot where my dad was the pastor. The church had a small front lawn that needed to be mowed every week. The grass was really nice Bermuda which always looked so green in the West Texas summer. I would mow the lawn every Saturday in preparation for Sunday morning church. I would edge the lawn and then sweep up all the grass

[20] James 3:9-12 (NKJV)

to make sure it looked perfect. I became very particular about how it looked. My dad would come over and inspect and he would always talk about how good I did. If someone made a comment about the lawn he would say, "Jon did that. Doesn't it look great?" Again, I am a sucker for words of affirmation. I haven't met many people who don't enjoy hearing words of affirmation.

Before I move on to the next chapter, let me share another story. I am currently forty-five years old and have a very obvious defense mechanism that shows up very often. I have been blessed to follow my dad's footsteps in ministry. I currently serve as the pastor of the church he pastored for twenty-two years. He is a godly man and very well loved by everyone. The older I get the more I appreciate him and the more I look like him. As I introduce him or he introduces me, people almost always say, "Wow! You two could not deny each other. You look just like your dad." In fact, this happened two days ago at church on Sunday. I responded the exact same way I do every time this happens. I said, "I know I can't deny him, my cars make it obvious." Everyone laughs and then the conversation begins. Why do I say that? I figure if I make fun of myself, then they can't. The deeper question is why do I feel as if they are going to make fun of me? Well, you probably know the answer. I remember like it was yesterday. I can still hear the words from the playground. I can still remember the smell of the barber shop. I can still picture the spinning blue and red sign outside the door. I believe I was in second grade when it happened. My parents were out of town and my Grandpa took me to the old-fashioned barber shop. I got the old crew cut. I was devastated. I didn't ask for it and I definitely didn't want it. I was already embarrassed by my big ears and had been made fun of many times. As I looked into the mirror, I knew what was going to be said the next day. I knew I was going to hear the comments about my ears and I was not looking forward to it. The power of those words still makes a forty-five year old man feel the need to mock himself before he can be mocked. I honestly laugh about my ears now, but don't think for a moment I don't still have painful memories of those words. Trust me, your words are powerful and lasting.

God wants you to use your words to direct and to delight. I have heard of the 5 to 1 principle. The 5 to 1 principle says we should say five positive comments to one negative comment. As we looked at earlier, negative words tend to stick longer and have more power. Be intentional as you speak to your children. Speak direction and delight into them every day. Let me give you twelve words that could change your relationship with your child and the direction of their life.

"I am proud of you,"

"I love you,"

"You are good at …"

Try saying these every day to your child and see what happens. I am sure you can think of a lot more, but here is a place to start.

CHAPTER 10
NO MÁS

The title of this chapter fulfills two purposes. The first reason is this is the last chapter. The second has to do with one of the most famous fights in boxing history. The fight is known as the *No Más Fight*. I began this book challenging you to fight for your family. I will close the book encouraging you to stay in the fight. In case you don't know, no más means *no more* in Spanish. Let me take a moment to explain the fight.

Sugar Ray Leonard vs Roberot Durán II, also known as the *No Más Fight* is one of the most famous fights in boxing history. It took place on November 25, 1980, at the Louisiana Superdome in New Orleans. This was the second of three bouts between these two legendary boxers. The fight is known as the *No Más Fight* because of what took place at the end of the eighth round. Durán turned away from Leonard towards the referee and quit by apparently saying, no más.

Durán has said that he never said the words no más to anyone following the bout. He blamed the broadcaster Howard Cosell for coming up with it and claiming he said it. He said he was only mumbling to himself, "No sigo, no sigo, no sigo", which translates to repeatedly saying, "I'm not going any further."[1]

He has said that he quit because of stomach cramps, which started to bother him in the fifth round. He said the cramps occurred because he took off weight too quickly, then ate too much after the morning weigh-in. However, his manager, Carolos Eleta, said Durán always ate that way before a fight. "Durán didn't quit because of stomach cramps," Eleta said, "He quit because he was embarrassed."[2]

Leonard claimed credit for having forced Durán to give up, and took great satisfaction in it. "I made him quit," Leonard said. "To make a man quit, to make Roberto Durán quit, was better than knocking him out."[3]

Please, don't quit. You will have good days and you will have bad days. You will have good seasons and bad

[1] "Roberto Durán tells the real story behind the 'No mas' bout," New York Daily News, August, 25, 2016, https://www.nydailynews.com/latino/roberto-duran-tells-real-story-behind-no-mas-bou-article-1.2765921.

[2] Dewey, Donald, *Ray Arcel: A Boxing Biography* (Jefferson, NC: McFarland, 2012), 175.

[3] William Nack, *Sports Illustrated,* December 8, 1980.

seasons. The great news is parenting is a life-long adven-
ture.

> You need to see parenting as one unending con-
> versation. As a parent, I find this mentality in-
> credibly freeing. Let me explain. You are freed
> from the pressure of needing to get from your
> child what you are never going to get in a single
> conversation. You know that this conversation is
> only one moment in an ongoing conversation that
> began when the child was born and will probably
> not end when your child leaves your home. You
> are liberated from having to load your hopes for
> your child into one conversation, because you
> know that you live with this child and you will
> get many more opportunities.[4]

In other words, your job never ends and you can never
give up. My kids are not kids anymore. However, parenting never ends; it simply evolves into something different.
Each stage of parenting brings with it new adventures and
new challenges. Each stage brings on a new opportunity
to trust that God loves your child more than you do. Each
stage brings a new opportunity to grow and experience
God's grace in a new way, through the lens of parenting.

[4] Paul David Tripp, *Parenting: The 15 Gospel Principles That Can
Radically Change Your Family* (Wheaton, IL: Crossway, 2016), 92.

"No other arena in life holds us more hostage to hope, more afraid to dream, more defensive about our decisions, and more open to receive help, all simultaneously."[5]

I have always loved sports. I have always been competitive. However, I have never been a runner. I don't have a runner's body, if you know what I mean. Ten years ago my brother ran a half-marathon and therefore I had to run a half-marathon. I trained for the half-marathon for nearly six months. I was thirty-five years old and in decent shape. I had never run that far though. The day of the race was finally upon me and I was very nervous and excited. I thought I was prepared, but I really wasn't. I live in Fort Worth and the race was the annual Cowtown Marathon. There were thousands of people running that day. I was almost late because of the traffic and because I was in such a hurry I didn't grab my long sleeve shirt. I had on shorts and the race t-shirt that I had gotten the day before. The temperature that day was in the thirties and there was a strong North wind. I ran to the starting line and immediately the gun sounded and we were off. We began running north and I was freezing. The marathon had several stages for me that day. There was the point of misery when I was freezing. Five miles into the race, the sun came out and then I felt perfect. Everyone else was shedding their clothes and

[5] Dan B Allender, *How Children Raise Parents: The Art of Listening to Your Family* (Colorado Springs, CO: Waterbrook, 2005), viii.

I was feeling very good about my decision to not wear a long-sleeved shirt. There was the excitement of running with thousands of other people. Then came the hill. I was not prepared for the hill. There was a mile-long bridge that went straight uphill. I had no idea we had that big of a hill in Fort Worth. Then there was the moment of relaxation. The joy of running with all of these people and accomplishing something I had never done before, and honestly never thought I could. The relaxation and enjoyment came to an end around mile ten or eleven. I thought I was going to die. I was certain I would never see the finish line. I thought I would be carried out on a stretcher. Interestingly enough, about that time I heard some weird person talking very loudly on his cell phone. I thought, who is this idiot who is talking on his phone during a half marathon on mile eleven. The voice got nearer and then it got more familiar. I looked over and realized I knew this moron. I said, "Hi" and we talked for a moment. He encouraged me to keep going and it seemed as if talking with him gave me the second or third wind that I needed. I pushed through the exhaustion and before I knew it, the sign said one more mile. The pain and exhaustion turned into an exhilarating feeling. As I neared the finish line, people were cheering and I felt a huge sense of accomplishment. I had done it. I had finished. I was proud of my achievement and somewhere I still have my medal. I was a little tired as I hurried back to church to coach my nephew's basketball game, but a lot proud.

I tell you this story because it sounds a lot like parenting. Many stages of parenting exist. Moments in which you feel like giving up and saying, "No más." There will be times in which you will not be able to contain your excitement for what your kids have accomplished. Those moments will be followed with a phone call that changes your perspective and you will feel utter despair. "The most humbling experience of life is being a parent, and at the same time, the most exhilarating experience is being a parent."[6]

No parent is perfect and no kid will be either. Make a commitment to fight for your family and when you make a mistake, keep fighting. The other day I was getting my haircut and the lady cutting my hair is about five months pregnant with her first child. She said she was nervous about parenting and wondered if she would be able to handle parenting. I told her "God is creating your child in your womb and He knows that you are the best mother for this child. He is giving you a child and He will enable you to be the best mother for this child." I told her," God has chosen you to raise this child, so you are the one who is

---

[6] Jim Burns, *Confident Parenting* (New Dehli: Good Times, 2010), 88-89.

best qualified to be the Mother." She said, "I guess I never thought about it that way, thank you."

Paul David Tripp puts it this way. "Nothing is more important in your life than being one of God's tools to form a human soul."[7] God has called you to be a parent. God has also equipped you to be a parent. God always equips those whom he calls. You may not feel qualified, but you are. You may not feel capable, but you are. You may not feel worthy, but you are. God has entrusted you with the gift of a life. Now it is your responsibility to train your child to love and follow Jesus. "God never calls you to a task without giving you what you need to do it. He never sends you without going with you."[8] Remember why you picked up this book in the first place. Remember why you continued to read this book. You made a choice to fight for your family. When parenting gets tough, and it often does, remember the words of Nehemiah and for God's sake fight.

Nehemiah 4:14

[14] And I looked, and arose and said to the nobles, to the leaders, and to the rest of the people, "Do not be afraid of them. Remember the Lord, great and awesome, and fight for your brethren,

---

[7] Tripp, *Parenting*, 21.
[8] Tripp, *Parenting*, 33.

your sons, your daughters, your wives, and your houses."[9]

Let me share with you one other passage of scripture before you go. The author of this Psalm encourages you as a parent to teach your children to love and follow the Lord. Read this as a reminder of your purpose. Remember, we will answer to God on how we raised our kids not on how they turned out.

Psalm 78:1-7

[1] An Asaph psalm Listen, dear friends, to God's truth, bend your ears to what I tell you. [2] I'm chewing on the morsel of a proverb; I'll let you in on the sweet old truths, [3] Stories we heard from our fathers, counsel we learned at our mother's knee. [4] We're not keeping this to ourselves, *we're passing it along to the next generation*—GOD's fame and fortune, the marvelous things he has done. [5] He planted a witness in Jacob, set his Word firmly in Israel, Then commanded our parents to teach it to their children [6] So the next generation would know, and all the generations to come—Know the truth and tell the stories so their children [7] can

---

[9] Nehemiah 4:14 (NKJV)

trust in God, Never forget the works of God but keep his commands to the letter.[10]

I am grateful you chose to read this book and I pray it will help you as you strive to raise kids to love and follow Jesus. Please, don't give up. Fight for your family and keep fighting. In the words of Robert Schneider, from the movie *Water Boy*, "You can do it!" Better yet listen to what the Lord told Joshua.

Joshua 1:9

Have I not commanded you? Be strong and of good courage; do not be afraid, nor be dismayed, for the LORD your God is with you wherever you go."[11]

God has entrusted you to train your child to love and follow Jesus. He will equip you to accomplish what He has called you to do. He is with you. He will give your strength. Rest in Him. He has got it. He has got you. He has got your child. Make the choice each day for the rest of your life to fight for your family.

[10] Psalm 78:1-7 (MSG) italics mine.
[11] Joshua 1:9 (NKJV)

Made in the USA
Monee, IL
27 August 2021